MORE PRAISE FOR *HIGH VELOCITY HIRING*

"*High Velocity Hiring* helps you look past the obvious, and often unseen, problems in your hiring process and focuses on the solutions that will work for your business. Scott Wintrip shapes a new way of managing the hiring process—a better, faster way—by identifying the barriers to fast, effective hiring and outlining specific ways to overcome them. The outcome for your organization will be a hiring process your hiring managers and your candidates can trust. I especially like the Seven Principles of an On-Demand System and how that awareness will help you prepare today for what you need tomorrow. That is, after all, the expectation of leaders everywhere. No one has a clearer view of how to improve your talent acquisition needs than Scott Wintrip."

—**Amy Ruth,** Senior Vice President, Human Services Group and Chief Human Resources Officer, Florida Blue

"*High Velocity Hiring* is a magnificent reminder of the power of hiring only the best talent. It illuminates wonderfully the principles of technique, process, and inventory building to help you make successful hires."

—**Angeles Valenciano,** Chief Executive Officer, National Diversity Council

"Understanding Hiring Styles, a key feature of *High Velocity Hiring*, is a game-changer when it comes to identifying top talent. Having worked with thousands of hiring managers across the country, I have been amazed when really smart leaders couldn't see or hear what I do. Over time I've realized that it's simply practice and a structured approach that helps avoid mismatches, and the fact we do this all day long has helped! Anyone who is unaware of hiring blindness and how their hiring style affects this issue will continue to make the same hiring mistakes."

—**Sharon Strauss,** Vice President of Client Services at Vitamin T

"We live in a new economy, what I call the Membership Economy. More than ever, buyers want to feel as though they are a part of something meaningful, while receiving great value for their investment. Turning ordinary customers into members for life requires companies to hire good people who do great work. *High Velocity Hiring* ensures that companies always have enough talented people to get the job done. I'm already recommending Scott's book to my clients."

—**Robbie Kellman Baxter,** Author of *The Membership Economy: Find Your Superusers, Master the Forever Transaction,* and *Build Recurring Revenue*

"Change is hard, and innovation doesn't always come easy. This seems especially true in hiring, as the leaders I work with tell me it seems harder than ever to find and retain good employees. Scott Wintrip's process in *High Velocity Hiring* is revolutionary. He clearly understands how empty seats undermine organizational effectiveness and has a proven process that eliminates this issue forever."

—**Seth Kahan,** Author of *Getting Innovation Right* and *Getting Change Right*

"Never before has a book made fast and accurate hiring so simple. *High Velocity Hiring* will permanently change how organizations find and select talented people worldwide."

—**Mark Levy,** Author of *Accidental Genius: Using Writing to Generate Your Best Ideas, Insight, and Content*

"Scott combines his passion for people with his well-earned hiring expertise to create a brilliant approach to make hiring simply effective."

—**Jay Perry,** Author of *Take Charge of Your Talent*

"Scott Wintrip reaffirms his fifth consecutive place on the Staffing 100 Most Influential People in the Staffing and Recruiting industry with *High Velocity Hiring: How to Hire Top Talent in an Instant.* Addressing why traditional hiring is broken, and how to solve the problem through engaging a new, innovative approach, Scott changes how the world hires, illustrating how to quickly fill open positions and keep them filled with quality employees."

—**Tammi Heaton,** Chief Operating Officer, PRIDESTAFF

"In *High Velocity Hiring*, Scott solves the most significant problem faced by all types of organizations across the globe—having the talent we need when we need it. Who better to have written this book than the guy who's driving the most important innovation in hiring?"

—**Pam O'Connor,** Consultant and Former Executive Vice President of HR, Catholic Relief Services

"Scott Wintrip decoded the process to eliminate the productivity drain of vacant positions. Every leader who has positions to fill will benefit greatly by focusing on the essentials of this process and learning to distinguish speed from haste."

—**Scott K. Edinger,** Author of *The Hidden Leader*

"In his book *High Velocity Hiring* Scott Wintrip has identified the most crucial considerations for executives seeking to identify and attract the right talent, quickly and cost-effectively. At a time when finding and obtaining talent comes at a premium, Scott has unlocked secrets that every organization needs to apply in order to grow and thrive in today's new economy."

—**Shawn Casemore,** Consultant, Speaker, and Author of *Operational Empowerment: Collaborate, Innovate, and Engage to Beat the Competition*

"I've always been baffled by long time-to-fill. Keeping a job open never makes sense, especially in our competitive world of business. Quality employees fuel growth and propel profitability. That's why *High Velocity Hiring* is so important. Every executive should read this book, and make it required reading of all managers throughout their company."

—**L. Allen Baker,** President and CEO, BG Staffing

"Scott articulates brilliantly in print what I have experienced from him so often in person; the clarity of a hugely significant problem statement addressed by a crystal-clear approach to resolving it. He backs his opinion and advice with well-researched, recognizable case studies that are easy to relate to, and then provides a systematic approach along with the encouragement and enthusiasm to help you succeed where others have failed. The only thing then between success and mediocrity is the leadership and mindset driving the change."

—**Mark Braund,** CEO, RedstoneConnect Plc.

"If I could make one change in all of the client organizations I work with, it would be the way they hire. I've seen the impact of long-empty roles and hires that don't work, and it can be devastating. Scott Wintrip offers a truly insightful approach to transforming hiring, starting most importantly from the mindset and building a process that ensures speed without haste. He combines his personal experience with data and lessons learned to offer the first really different view on the most important thing organizations do."

—**Karen Wright,** author of *The Complete Executive: The 10-Step System for Great Leadership Performance*

"In the dozen-plus years that I've known him, Scott Wintrip has consistently proved to be an expansive and innovative thought leader in his approach to recruiting, staffing, and hiring. His new book, *High Velocity Hiring*, reveals his groundbreaking process that allows business leaders to quickly hire top talent. I've been privileged to use Scott's counsel with great success; I'm eager to employ more of his insights to take hiring at my company to a whole new level."

—**Paula Roy,** Vice President, Human Resources, Alex Apparel Group, New York, NY

"Research-driven and pragmatic, Scott Wintrip boils down 30 years of hard-earned lessons on hiring into an interesting and digestible process for business owners, HR leaders, and recruiting professionals alike. He's taken the often reactive and suboptimal way most of us hire and turned it into a proactive, repeatable process critical for all growing businesses. As a result, the new world of talent engagement just got a playbook."

—**Eric Gregg,** Founder and CEO, Inavero

"With the pace of today's workplace only getting faster, HR and recruiters need to keep up. Using the 'tried and true' approach will only keep you lagging behind. A shift is needed, and Scott Wintrip's *High Velocity Hiring* approach does just that. This new way of thinking is relevant, needed, and applicable. Make the shift into high gear!"

—**Steve Browne,** SHRM-SCP, Executive Director of HR, LaRosa's, Inc.

"Being an entrepreneur and the founder of my company, one of the key challenges I face is attracting the best talent to propel my organization into the future. I've been following Scott Wintrip's wisdom for many years, and when it comes to the most unique, innovative, and breakthrough ideas, Scott is the most insightful thought leader and the leading authority in this field. Attracting and building an extraordinary team becomes your competitive advantage, your secret weapon, and your way of creating and controlling your future. *High Velocity Hiring* is the absolute blueprint on developing the proper mindset and what you need to do in order to create your dream team!"

—**Chad Barr,** President of The Chad Barr Group, Coauthor of *Million Dollar Web Presence*

"Your company's future depends on hiring the right talent. Scott Wintrip's new book is an invaluable resource to help you land top performers—even in crowded and competitive markets. *High Velocity Hiring* can become your company's secret weapon."

—**Dorie Clark,** author of *Reinventing You* and *Stand Out*, and Adjunct Professor at Duke University's Fuqua School of Business

"Scott Wintrip's book is exactly on point for today's economy, especially in a tight labor market that is only going to get tighter. Chapter 2 on the Talent Accelerator Process and Chapter 11 on Durable Diversity are two items every organization needs to be paying attention to as these are especially critical issues. Labor issues could easily determine your success and growth in the years to come."

—**Dr. Alan Beaulieu,** Principal and
Senior Economist, ITR Economics

"There's a big difference between speed and haste. Rather than make hasty hiring decisions, at IBM we have baked speed into our process for talent acquisition. That's why *High Velocity Hiring* is so important. Fast and accurate hiring is never an accident. It happens because leaders plan for it, implement a process to achieve it, and hold staff accountable to following the plan."

—**Obed Louissaint,** Vice President of
People and Culture for IBM Watson

"Talent is what differentiates organizations, and the best talent will always be the hallmark of the best organizations. Quickly finding and retaining talent is a must, and *High Velocity Hiring* offers proven and surprisingly potent ways to radically shrink time-to-fill so you can find and keep the right talent for your organization."

—**Amy Dufrane,** CEO, HR Certification Institute

"Scott Wintrip's innovative text, *High Velocity Hiring*, is an essential read (and frequent reference) for any organization striving to be best-in-class."

—**Neil Goldenberg,** MD, PhD, Associate Professor
of Pediatrics at Johns Hopkins University
School of Medicine, and Director of Research
at Johns Hopkins All Children's Hospital

"Successful leadership hinges upon surrounding yourself with talented people. You can't afford to wade through a long, drawn-out hiring process, nor can you risk making a bad hire. *High Velocity Hiring* shows you how to engage in fast and accurate hiring."

—**Lisa Earle McLeod,** author of *Leading with
Noble Purpose* and *Selling with Noble Purpose*

HIGH VELOCITY HIRING

HOW TO HIRE TOP TALENT IN AN INSTANT

SCOTT WINTRIP

New York Chicago San Francisco Athens London Madrid
Mexico City Milan New Delhi Singapore Sydney Toronto

1 2 3 4 5 6 7 8 9 0   LCR   21 20 19 18 17

ISBN: 978-1-259-85947-2
MHID: 1-259-85947-9

e-ISBN: 978-1-259-85948-9
e-MHID: 0-1-259-859948-7

McGraw-Hill Education books are available at special quantity discounts to use as premiums and sales promotions, or for use in corporate training programs. To contact a representative, please visit the Contact Us page at www.mhprofessional.com.

Dedicated to the companies I've been honored to serve.
Thank you for your trust.

CONTENTS

ACKNOWLEDGMENTS

Writing *High Velocity Hiring* has been a goal of mine for over a decade. When time-to-fill hit its highest point in 15 years in 2015, I knew it was time.

In the book, I mention the village of people who influenced my children. I've had my own village, without whom this book wouldn't have been possible.

I'm grateful for the opportunity to work with my editor at McGraw-Hill, Donya Dickerson. She immediately embraced this project, knowing from her own experience the importance of the new way of hiring. Her insights, along with the work of the team at McGraw-Hill, have helped shape the ideas I wanted to share. I'm also grateful to the sales and marketing teams at McGraw-Hill for getting this book into the hands of people who will benefit from it.

Special thanks to my literary agent, Ted Weinstein. His input was invaluable, especially in helping translate my experience into a practical guide for readers. I've told Ted that if he ever wants to change careers, he'd make a great recruiter. However, given his skill as a literary agent, publishing can't afford to lose him.

A big "thank you" to Mark Levy. Mark was combination muse and sounding board as I wrote this book. Working with Mark is unique—we'd jump on Skype, discussing each chapter. This helped develop content and got me through some of those lonely days as writer. To say that Mark is amazing at his work doesn't do him justice.

A special shoutout to my clients. I'm grateful to have served organizations across the globe. Many of the leaders I've worked with have joked that I'm like their therapist, letting them safely vent their frustration. I've always appreciated the underlying compliment in this statement. I'm honored to have done business with so many outstanding organizations.

A huge "thank you" to those I interviewed for the book. These leaders have given a gift to readers by sharing their experiences. Also, my thanks to the associations and research firms who contributed their data and insights.

My village also includes friends, work colleagues, and mentors who've been incredibly supportive as I've worked on this project. Special thanks to the 628 and BSS groups for their belief in me and my work. A pat on the back for Tom, Jack, and John for being excellent role models and dear friends. Also, thanks to Bill, my most important mentor.

Lastly, I'm fortunate to have a loving family that makes me a better person. This includes my Mom and Dad, who showed me the importance of accountability. My son, Benjamin, and "bonus" daughter, Mackenzie, who I kept in mind as I was writing. I hope they'll always have great employers who practice the principles I've outlined in the book. And Holly, my wife, to whom I'm so blessed to be married. My favorite part of this book will always be the story of how we met.

If I've overlooked anyone, I apologize. Please know that any oversights are mine, and mine alone.

Why Hiring Is Broken

We've all heard it said that a company's most important asset is its people. When we say we love a company, what we're really saying is we love the work being done by the people in that company. People are the reason why Apple, Alphabet (Google), Amazon.com, and Starbucks remain some of the world's most admired companies.[1] That's why hiring the right employees is so important. Good employees who do outstanding work make their companies great.

Because of this extreme importance of people, hiring has long been rooted in fear—fear of getting it wrong. Making a mistake can be costly. A bad hire can undermine a department, delay a project, and damage the reputation of the hiring manager. The damage doesn't stop there.

According to the Society for Human Resource Management (SHRM), a hiring mistake could cost up to five times the bad hire's annual salary.[2] Also, a majority of chief financial officers surveyed by global staffing firm Robert Half suggests the biggest cost of a bad hire might not be financial. They ranked degraded staff morale and a drop in productivity as more significant issues.[3]

To ensure they have the right people, leaders have been encouraged to be "slow to hire and quick to fire." They've adopted interviewing techniques that look at past behavior as a predictor of future performance. They've also employed testing and technologies to measure skills, analyze personalities, and assess honesty and integrity. One or two rounds of interviews with prospective job candidates have expanded into three, four, or even five rounds. As a result of these intensive and expanded efforts, filling one job can take weeks or months—all in an effort to get it right the first time.

This standard approach (keeping a job open until the right person shows up) has a big downside. In an organization, an empty seat is like an open wound. It's a painful distraction that interferes with the business's core mission. The department manager has to manage the extra workload. HR has to add one more task to its already overflowing plate. The talent acquisition team has to scramble to fill one more open job, made harder because of a skills shortage. With every passing day, overtime pay builds up, as do hiring costs.

Finding enough qualified candidates to interview can take weeks or months. Once they begin, the multiple rounds of interviews are often followed by testing, reference checking, and background checks. Finally, if all goes well, an offer is made to the most qualified person. However, if that offer is rejected and the second choice candidate has already moved on, the process starts all over again, adding more time, more effort, more expense, more overtime, more interviews.

Has slow to hire and quick to fire worked? Not if you're a leader with an unfilled job. Certainly not if you're in HR and can't find enough qualified people. Definitely not if you're in talent acquisition, and your best candidate was hired by a faster competitor. Time-to-fill (the length of time it takes to fill a job) is at an all-time high (Figure Intro.1),[4] and there's been no improvement to employee turnover.[5]

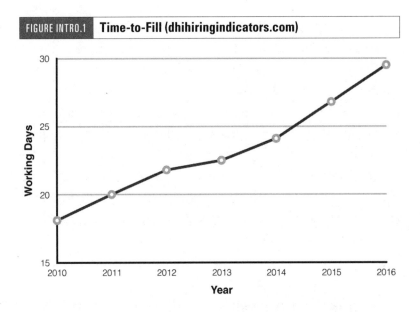

FIGURE INTRO.1 | **Time-to-Fill (dhihiringindicators.com)**

The world operates on a faulty premise: People equate time and effort spent on hiring with making a quality hire. The more time they take, the more energy they expend, the better the hire will be. It gives them a false sense of control. Taking lots of time to hire doesn't save companies from bad hires; it only saves people from making a decision they're afraid may be wrong. It's not that these are bad people. They simply have bought into a bad idea. The old way of hiring is to keep a job open until the right person shows up. It's created long time-to-fill, lots of open seats, higher expenses, added effort, and frustrated leaders.

Hiring is broken, and that's why I wrote this book. There's a new way to hire that's faster, efficient, and effective. Instead of waiting for the right *person* to show up, the new way to hire is to wait for the right *job* to show up. Instead of waiting until a seat is empty to search for talent, the new way of hiring starts the talent search before that job opens. Rather than recruiting from behind, it requires that leaders plan ahead, lining up talented people before they are needed.

The importance of having talented people in each role exactly when they're needed makes the new way of hiring a strategic imperative. Everyone involved in employee selection—executives, hiring managers, HR, and recruiters—is part of an efficient process that fills jobs the day they become open.

If you're thinking this sounds too simple or too good to be true, you're not alone. That's a common reaction—that is, until you look at how the rest of the world has gotten much faster, and how those lessons apply to hiring.

Choosing to Be Fast

It wasn't that long ago that simple, everyday tasks took an hour, a day, or longer. The process of booking a trip began with calling a travel agent, who researched options, called us back, and then booked the trip for us. Today, we can book that flight ourselves in a matter of minutes. Depositing checks meant getting in the car, driving to bank, waiting in line, and handing those checks to a bank teller. With mobile banking, we can make those same deposits from our desk in a matter of seconds. Developing photos used to require mailing the roll of film to a processor or dropping it off at the one-hour photo store. Now, we can instantly view those photos on our cameras or smartphones and immediately print them at home.

Being faster than competitors, without sacrificing quality and accuracy, has given a growing number of companies a distinct, competitive edge. Take for example sandwich shops, arguably one of the most oversaturated segments of the restaurant trade. In 1983, then 19-year-old Jimmy John Liautaud opened his first sandwich shop in Charleston, Illinois. Offering delivery of his sandwiches made his shop popular. As the company grew, Jimmy John's made a choice not just to deliver but to do so faster than competitors, what they refer to as "freaky fast delivery."[6] Their commitment to providing a quality product with speed has paid off, elevating Jimmy John's to the number-one spot on *Entrepreneur* magazine's list of top 500 franchises.[7]

Getting something fast used to mean sacrificing quality. Accuracy once required time and lots of patience. Today, more of what we need or want can be acquired right now or just minutes from now. From downloads to deliveries to services on command, the rise of the on-demand economy has made speed a requirement for doing business, not just a competitive advantage. The development of the process that drives the on-demand economy demonstrates that speed, quality, and accuracy are not mutually exclusive.

This brings us to an important question: What happens when you apply the process for the on-demand delivery of products and services to hiring? The answer: You get organizations that can fill their jobs in less than an hour. Throughout the book, you'll learn how companies across the globe have applied the principles of the on-demand economy to hiring. You'll gain a step-by-step process for implementing fast and accurate hiring of quality employees in your company. Also, you'll discover consequences that many find surprising: Hiring faster creates better employees and improved working relationships.

How I Developed High Velocity Hiring

My involvement with High Velocity Hiring started when I was 16 years old and looking for my first job. I went door to door, visiting the businesses all around my Canton, Ohio, neighborhood. I asked for a job at a florist, a dry cleaner, a car dealer, and a few convenience stores. I even asked for a job at a funeral home. I heard variations of the same "no." It wasn't until I got to a little mom-and-pop restaurant, The Sandwich and Waffle Shop, that I was hired as a busboy on the spot. I, of course, was thrilled and assumed that this was how all businesses hired—quickly and decisively. This belief was reinforced in my first year of college, when I applied to work in a manufacturing plant and was hired that same day.

A few years later, I began my career as a recruiter. That wasn't my original plan. In college, I was a music major who wanted to become a high school band director. I learned about recruiting when I went to an employment agency, looking to earn extra money. During the interview, the office manager asked if I'd ever considered a job in the staffing industry. I didn't know there was such an industry. While I didn't accept her offer, it did plant a seed. That I could earn a living matching people and jobs seemed like a meaningful career. Within a few months, I sought out my first staffing job. It came with what I thought was a highly impressive title—executive search consultant.

As I began my tenure in recruiting, I discovered that the instantaneous hiring I had experienced was far from the norm. At the employers I contacted, jobs had frequently been open for weeks, months, and sometimes years. Often, these jobs weren't open because of a lack of candidates. The companies had already interviewed dozens of people, some of whom were well qualified. However, they weren't hired, even though that empty seat was delaying projects, creating missed opportunities, and costing lots of overtime. These companies allowed the process to drag on and on.

These hiring delays were also affecting job candidates. Many were already working full-time jobs and had little time to deal with a drawn-out hiring process. In some cases, I watched qualified candidates grow so frustrated that they abandoned their search. Rather than tolerate an inefficient, prolonged job search that may or may not improve their circumstances, they chose to stick it out with their current employers—even when their current jobs were not meeting their needs.

I saw this as an opportunity. Yes, this was about doing the greater good and facilitating a process where the needs of all parties were met quickly. Just as important, I felt like I had found my purpose. I had always wanted to make a difference, which is one of the reasons I wanted to be a teacher. What I never expected is that I would be teaching people a new way of hiring. Was this easy? Heavens no! I was working against the status quo. I had to have talent ready to go, encourage hiring managers to act quickly, and then keep the process moving forward.

The payoff of being an on-demand provider of talent became clear quickly. One of my favorite examples is that of a manufacturer in North Carolina. Their information technology department needed a leader. Based upon their previous experiences with recruiters, they thought it would take months to find the correct person. However, since I had cultivated a Talent Inventory, my "warehouse" of people that were ready to go, that wasn't the case. I told them about Mark, a candidate in my warehouse, who they hired the very next day. That was more than two decades ago, and Mark is still there, reinforcing for me that rapid hiring can be done immediately and accurately. In fact, he was promoted to chief technology officer and plans on retiring there—unless he gets an unexpected call from NASA.

Watching the ongoing, positive impact that this approach was having in the companies I led inspired me to share this with a broader audience. That is why I became a business advisor and consultant, creating the Wintrip Consulting Group in 1999. Since then, I've been honored to work with companies across the globe, helping them to implement a process that allows them to hire in an instant: The very same process you'll learn about, in detail, in this book.

You'll also read about the impact an on-demand approach to hiring has had for companies both large and small, including:

- Why a financial institution was able to recruit more top talent than they could ever hire

- How a technology company improved new-hire success by over 90 percent

- Why a hospital could fill open nursing jobs in less than an hour

- How a manufacturer eliminated turnover for its most critical roles

Having now shared this expertise with thousands of companies, and tens of thousands of their employees, I know that, together, we have impacted the lives of hundreds of thousands of people who have gone to work faster, improving their lives and circumstances along the way. All the while, those companies have become better organizations that achieved improved revenue, higher employer retention, and greater market share, just to name a few of the many positive results.

How This Book Is Structured

In Chapter 1 we'll explore the primary cause of open jobs and long time-to-fill, along with beliefs and common recruiting and hiring methods that keep people stuck in the status quo. Chapter 2 begins our focus on eliminating these causes of inefficient hiring. We'll look at the rise of the on-demand economy and how we can apply its core principles to filling jobs. Chapters 3 through 8 detail the steps of the Talent Accelerator Process (TAP), the method you'll use to engage in High Velocity Hiring:

- **Step #1—Create Hire-Right Profiles:** You'll learn how to create detailed blueprints of who's the best fit for a job.

- **Step #2—Improve Candidate Gravity:** To draw a better flow of top talent that matches each Hire-Right Profile, you'll discover how to assess and improve the attractive force your company has on potential employees.

- **Step #3—Maximize Hiring Styles:** To counteract hiring blindness, a psychological phenomenon that narrows perceptive ability and causes hiring mistakes, I'll illustrate how to create hiring teams comprised of four complementary hiring styles.

- **Step #4—Conduct Experiential Interviews:** You'll learn how to conduct experiential interviews, allowing you to gain absolute proof that a candidate either does or does not fit the needs of your company.

- **Step #5—Maintain a Talent Inventory:** To ensure that jobs can be filled the instant they open, you'll discover how to build and maintain a supply of people ready to be hired the moment they are needed.

- **Step #6—Keep the TAP Flowing:** You'll learn what can interfere with the new way of hiring, and gain methods to ensure you can always hire in an instant.

Chapter 9 explains how to improve hiring efficiency using automation. In Chapter 10, you'll learn how to partner with the best external talent scouts. Chapter 11 shows you how to use the Talent Accelerator Process to sustain a diverse workforce.

Throughout the book, I've included stories about leaders and organizations across the globe. In many instances, I mention the leader by first name only, and I describe their organization without identifying it explicitly. This was done either at their request or to protect confidentiality.

At the end of every chapter, you'll find a list of suggested action steps. These will help you implement the ideas you'll be reading. I recommend bookmarking these pages, as they will serve as a ready reference that you'll want to review often.

Before we begin, I want to say "thank you," but not just for buying this book. How your organization finds and selects people is the most important part of your business strategy. Your involvement in the hiring process impacts the most important asset of your company and is a very important part of people's lives. Thank you for the work you do each day. By making the hiring process faster and more accurate, your organization will have talented people instead of empty seats. The people in those seats will have faster access to the resources they need to live their lives and support their families. Now, together, let's get started so you can hire in an instant.

The Emperor Has No Talent

What Causes Long Time-to-Fill?

Why does it take some companies weeks or months to fill just one job? Maybe it's the companies' reputation if they're known as bad places to work. Possibly, it's their location if they're situated in a part of town that's difficult to reach. Also, it could be an undesirable work environment, low pay, or a benefits package that's lousy. While one or more of these issues can be a factor in attracting quality candidates, most companies blame long time-to-fill on a shortage of available talent. However, available talent is not the real problem.

Some companies fill their open seats with relative ease and speed, even though there are more jobs than people to fill them. What makes these organizations truly different isn't their reputation, location, work environment, or pay and benefits. It's *how* they've chosen to address the talent shortage. They recognize that the old way of hiring— keeping a job open until the right person shows up—doesn't work when there's a people shortage. The leaders in these companies understand that a reactive process doesn't work, and that the old way of hiring resulted from having the wrong mindset.

Today, these leaders and their companies engage in the new way of hiring by *actively cultivating top talent and then waiting for the right job to open.* They've acknowledged that there's always a shortage of talent, which requires a shift in thinking and a permanent change in hiring strategy.

The Perpetual Talent Shortage

For years, the media has bombarded us with stories about the skills shortage. Not enough people have been available to manage the volumes of data being crunched by businesses.[1] A scarcity of welders, electricians, and machinists has hampered manufacturers.[2] Companies have struggled to fill openings for sales reps, teachers, and nurses.[3] The talent shortage has also slowed construction of new homes.[4]

Contrary to common belief, talent shortages even persist during economic downturns. During the Great Recession, there was still a disparity between open jobs and qualified people to fill them. An October 2008 report by CNN indicated that a "shortage of qualified workers continues to impact employers with 59 percent of hiring managers citing it as their primary recruiting challenge."[5]

The United States wasn't the only country experiencing shortages of skilled workers in the midst of the Great Recession. Japan was running out of engineers,[6] and Australia didn't have enough lawyers.[7] The automotive industry listed the lack of skilled talent as its biggest business concern in both India and China.[8] In the United Kingdom, there was a shortage of sheep shearers.[9]

The talent deficit isn't only real; it's pervasive across all industries. Having been involved in hiring for three decades, I've watched companies struggle to fill open jobs in good times and bad. These struggles aren't limited to small or obscure companies. The biggest, most resourceful corporations experience major recruiting challenges. That's one reason why nearly all of the Fortune 500 has relied on outside agencies to procure workers. Contingent workers on temporary and contract assignments made up 18 percent of the workforce in large companies in 2015.[10]

While technology has improved some aspects of hiring, it hasn't eliminated open jobs and lengthy hiring delays. The Internet, in particular, has leveled the playing field. Your company and all of your competitors can reach out to top talent. Candidates also have easier access to you. They often apply for lots of jobs, including ones for which they're ill suited. This creates a flood of resumes, many of which won't fit your needs. A robust recruiting effort, such as this, used to be available only to large organizations; now small companies can mount a campaign that steers more candidates their way. Highly qualified candidates have many choices, including the option of doing their own thing by joining the "gig economy" as freelancers. Technology has actually magnified the skills shortage, straining a talent pool that is nearly tapped out.

The problem isn't people. There have never been enough qualified candidates to go around. That's a fact that isn't going to change. Ongoing innovations will constantly create a vacuum for new skills. The Internet's availability as a hiring tool will continue to expand, creating increased demand for the finite supply of talent. People will gain more options for how they choose to work, further diminishing the availability of candidates for full-time jobs. As globalization increases, borders will matter less, creating a talent competition unlike anything we've seen before.

The real problem is process. Most companies keep a job open until the right person shows up. These companies are stuck in the old way. It's not that they don't want to hire differently; it's that they don't know how.

The Damaging Impact of the Scarcity Mindset

Yes, the shortage of talent makes hiring difficult, especially when you engage in the old way of hiring. If you're like most leaders, you want to hire differently. However, it's hard to think your way out of this problem. Especially when you're facing odds that appear insurmountable.

Watch almost any sport and you'll easily see the impact of a negative mindset. When one team racks up goal after goal, the other team loses steam. The bigger the scoring gap, the harder it becomes for the losing team to compete. As the winning club dominates, the other side forgets their plays and makes mistakes. The players on the losing team can't seem to keep their heads in the game.

Mindset matters a lot. A scoreboard, whether it's tracking results in sports or monitoring hiring statistics in corporate life, can trigger negative thinking. Add to this persistent bad news, such as all of the ongoing press coverage of skills shortages, and it's normal that you'd be concerned, even fearful, about your prospects of finding the talented people you need for your jobs. These negative emotions not only make work stressful, they actually undermine your resourcefulness.

In her research on emotions and positive psychology, Barbara Fredrickson found that positive emotions lead to more expansive and creative behavior. Fredrickson's work has demonstrated that "people's daily experiences of positive emotions compound over time to build a variety of consequential personal resources."[11] Negative emotions, in turn, limit resourcefulness.

In field experiments, Fredrickson documented evidence that demonstrates that positive emotions place people on trajectories of growth. Called the "broaden-and-build" theory, these trajectories build resourcefulness in areas including pathways thinking (believing that goals can be attained by one's own resources), environmental mastery (the sense that we are able to have an influence on the events in our lives), and ego-resilience (the ability to adapt to different situations and respond accordingly).[12]

That's why the hyperfocus on a shortage of skills is so problematic. The ongoing negative press paints a dark picture that is continually reinforced by the numbers. While all of the news and numbers are meant to inform, there's an unfortunate side-effect: They wear you down. Bad news and numbers engender negative emotions, draining your resourcefulness. Instead of being on a trajectory of growth, you get stuck, often feeling powerless to effect lasting change. Rather than seeing goals as opportunities that can be attained by your own resources, goals can appear to be unattainable or unrealistic. And forget about being able to adapt to different situations, especially when everything, including the numbers, seems stacked against you. How many times have we been told that the numbers don't lie?

Over the past three decades, I've witnessed firsthand the increasingly debilitating effects of the skills shortages. Smart leaders who previously had demonstrated incredible acumen at problem-solving were suddenly stuck, unable to solve this hiring conundrum. Organizations that, for years, were able to attract droves of job candidates based upon reputation alone were now experiencing a mere trickle of talented people. Professional recruiters in corporations and outside agencies have also been impacted, as they've tried to fill what seems like an ever-increasing number of jobs with a perpetually decreasing pool of people.

Sound familiar? You've likely experienced one or more of these negative impacts of the skills shortage. That's the problem with scarcity. Shortfalls of talent make recruiting a challenge for everyone. Adding to this challenge are the damaging impacts that talent scarcity has on your psyche. Believing that the odds are stacked against you makes it difficult to solve a problem. This has certainly been the case with jobs that are especially hard to fill.

Numbers Don't Lie

Finding good software developers can be difficult. If you're in San Jose, California, the heart of Silicon Valley, it may seem impossible. Especially when you look at the numbers. From September 2015 through February 2016, there were 54,250 open software developer jobs in San Jose. Compare that to the active supply of candidates available to fill those jobs—just 4,408.[13]

Two of the companies competing for these software developers have been battling over talent for decades. The larger of the two is a well-known technology company with thousands of employees. Having a reputation for developing high-quality products, the company gets great press for its innovative approaches. On Glassdoor.com, a job and recruiting site with millions of employer reviews, people give the company high marks. Positive comments praise the corporate environment and engaging work, the talented colleagues whom the company hires, and their easily accessible location. Having a great story to tell, the talent acquisition department employs numerous methods for drawing in potential new hires, including formalized referral programs, postings on job boards, a robust website to draw in applicants, and live and virtual open houses.

The other company is smaller in size, isn't as well known, and, as a result, gets less press coverage—much less. Their products receive decent reviews; some people like them while others do not. Comments on Glassdoor offer faint praise for the work environment and numerous complaints about the location of the facility and the lack of advancement opportunities. Their talent acquisition team, if you can really call it that, comprises the staff in HR, who also perform all of the other tasks you might expect of a human resources department, including onboarding new hires, managing benefits, and processing endless piles of employee paperwork. Like the larger firm, they use multiple methods for drawing in talent, including job boards, referral generation, their own website, and a few open houses each year. However, the smaller size of their HR team limits the time they can devote to these tools.

It's reasonable to expect that the larger company would have more success in recruiting talented candidates. Their all-around better circumstances should provide the means and the motivation to do better. The talent acquisition team can take great pride in sharing their story as they leverage the wealth of recruiting resources at their disposal.

It's also reasonable to expect that the smaller firm would always be one step behind, scrambling to grab second- or third-tier leftover talent. However, that's not the case. Like a short, nerdy kid who surprises everyone when he knocks down a bully, the smaller firm has been winning the talent battle, beating the bigger company year after year. Why? Because their leaders treat the skills shortage as though it were a myth.

Numbers Don't Lie, But Do Deceive

"As far as our leadership team is concerned, there isn't a talent shortage," said Donald, CEO of the smaller technology firm. "In fact, we've made saying the words 'skills shortage' or any other phrase that implies that idea a fire-able offense." Things weren't always like this at Donald's company, where's he's served as the CEO for a decade.

In 2005, the company was experiencing what they termed a "talent crisis of epic proportions." According to Donald, "Our flow of viable candidates had decreased substantially. When our team had people to interview, those interviews took too long and weren't all that effective. We had too many open jobs and not enough people to fill them."

The company had experimented with a variety of solutions. These included a yearlong stint with a Vendor Management System (an Internet-based solution for businesses to manage and procure staffing services), incorporating Topgrading (a corporate hiring and interviewing methodology), and a brief experiment with Recruitment Process Outsourcing (the employer transfers all or part of its recruitment processes to an external service provider). While these different initiatives helped the company fill some jobs somewhat faster, overall time-to-fill continued to increase. "It's not that any of these methods were wrong or bad," said Donald. "They just weren't solving our persistent hiring problems."

I first met Donald at a conference I keynoted. Following my speech, he asked to meet in the hotel bar to discuss how I might help his company. Drink in hand, Donald vented his frustration about the talent shortage and how it was hampering their efforts to fill open seats and reduce time-to-fill. According to him, their competitors, especially bigger companies, were "snapping up all of the good software developers." Walking me through the litany of solutions they had tried, he was openly incredulous that I had somehow created a different method that allowed companies to fill jobs in an instant. "Look," he told me, "it was a nice speech, but I just can't believe it's that easy."

Having heard this many times before, I simply smiled, acknowledging that Donald was not alone in his doubts. Then, I asked him, "Donald whose jobs is your company trying to fill?" Looking at me as if I'd lost my mind, he said with a tinge of sarcasm, "Seriously? Do I have to answer that? Of course we're focused on ours." I replied, "Then why are you so concerned about everyone else's too?" Donald immediately started to respond, but pulled up short. I could almost see his mental wheels turning.

Like many leaders, Donald and his team were overly focused on the numbers, especially that there were more jobs than skilled people to fill them. However, their company isn't trying to fill all of those jobs, just their own. That's why my question created his pause—he, like most leaders, hadn't looked at the numbers in that context.

After nearly a minute of silence, Donald talked through an epiphany. "You know what, you're right. Our leadership team, myself included, has spent too long and has been too focused on skills shortages. Yes, mathematically speaking, there are more jobs than people. But, those numbers are deceiving. Our leadership team has always been great at solving problems when we get out of the problem and into solutions. That's how you've helped companies implement a process that lets them fill jobs in an instant, isn't it, Scott? We simply need a strategy that allows us to fill our jobs the moment they open."

A shift in thinking is the first step you need to take to hire faster, which was certainly the case for Donald and his team. After hiring me as their advisor, our conversations focused on solving their specific hiring challenges (versus staying stuck in the problem, blaming the talent shortage for their woes). Donald's first directive was to ban conversations about skills or talent shortages, focusing everyone instead on how their company was going to be an exception to the negative statistics. Together, we created a plan that allowed the company to fill their software developer openings in an instant. From there, we expanded the process to include additional jobs as the HR department and hiring managers got better at executing the plan.

As momentum increased, we could see Fredrickson's broaden-and-build theory in action. Everyone involved in hiring was becoming visibly resourceful, believing they had enough resources to hire quickly and accurately. As the initiative progressed, both hiring managers and the HR team adapted to changing circumstances, learning from those situations versus being a victim of them. This trajectory of growth and success made their smaller size and limited resources irrelevant. Their time-to-fill plummeted while that of other companies, including that bigger competitor, continued to climb. In less than a year, they turned their talent crisis of epic proportions into a talent surplus.

Looking back at their progress, Donald acknowledged that there really was a shortage. "For too long, we allowed all the reports on talent shortages to consume us, instead of just inform us. But not anymore. Our team has proven there is sufficient talent as long as we follow our process to attract and hire the best people. We discovered the real shortage wasn't talent. What we lacked was a process that focused our mindset and efforts."

The Process Problem

While the global talent shortage is an ongoing reality, it's not really your problem. After all, your company isn't responsible for filling all the world's open jobs. The only jobs you need to fill are your own. That shift in thinking puts the skills shortage in a perspective that's manageable. Rather than being a pervasive problem, the skills shortage is merely a challenge that can be solved by a better process.

The critical problem—the only one you can control—is having the right kind of hiring process. The right process taps into a sufficient pool of talent and efficiently moves candidates toward hire.

"Quite often, long time-to-fill can be traced to the selection process," said Rob McIntosh, chief analyst for ERE Media, an information services provider that measures important hiring data at dozens of large organizations. ERE found that, even after recruiters identified candidates for open jobs, many of these organizations continued to experience hiring delays. Why? The trouble was with the hiring managers. They were taking too long to hire. Even when they were presented with a dozen qualified candidates, the managers would take days or weeks to pull the trigger.

If you want to eliminate empty seats and reduce time-to-fill, you have to address the problem in its entirety. You have to change both your mindset and process. Instead of focusing on talent scarcity, you must adopt a belief in *talent sufficiency*: That the right approach will generate enough qualified people to fill open jobs. Since speed is essential, you have to require everyone involved in the selection process to think nimbly and act swiftly. The methods that comprise the process must address all the factors slowing down fast hiring. Then, and only then, can your organization hire in an instant.

More on Mindsets

That the world has a skills shortage is a reality. That the skills shortage should hinder your hiring efforts is a belief. Rather, it's a convenient excuse that does nothing to solve the problem.

Talent scarcity isn't the only detrimental belief or mindset. Several additional counterproductive mindsets, all rooted in fear, remain pervasive:

"You must be slow to hire and quick to fire."

People who are slow to hire operate out of fear—the fear of making a bad choice. They've experienced the consequences of poor hiring choices, and as a way to avoid these consequences, they overcompensate by slowing down the process. To keep from making a bad decision, they avoid making one at all, believing that speed and accuracy are mutually exclusive. This plodding approach to employee selection causes overanalysis and a protracted timeline. Talented candidates move on and open jobs remain open.

"This is how it's always been done, so it must be right."

At Donald's company there was an unwritten rule: For each open job, the hiring manager had to review a slate of eight to ten candidates. When I asked why, I was told, "This is how it's always been done." This rule not only slowed down hiring, it didn't serve any necessary function. After implementing more efficient methods, leaders were able to make better hires after considering only a candidate or two.

(continued)

Many organizations keep doing things the same way, even when that way is ineffective. It's easier to maintain the status quo, especially if you're afraid that changing things won't work. Doing "business as usual" keeps companies stuck in the slow lane of hiring, losing valuable time and top talent to faster competitors.

"The odds are good that the goods are odd."

One of Donald's must trusted senior vice presidents was Marcus. After a series of disastrous hires, Marcus added additional interviews and expanded background checks to an already lengthy process. His assumption was that most candidates were flawed, prompting his comment that "the odds are good that the goods are odd." The only flaw was in Marcus' thinking. Past experience had skewed Marcus' mindset, compromising his objectivity. He failed to see that the problem wasn't bad candidates, but that some people are a bad fit for a job.

Most leaders end up making some hiring decisions they later regret. As a result, they often err on the side of caution by attempting to avoid similar mistakes. This fear leads to added steps, creating a longer process.

What Slows Fast Hiring?

The key to speed is having an efficient process—one that eliminates the three main hiring obstacles. Let's look at each obstacle, one at a time.

Obstacle #1: Tapping Into a Candidate Pool That's Too Small

If you asked employers why they can't fill jobs, over a third will tell you they're not getting enough applicants, or they're getting

FIGURE 1.1	Untapped Talent Pools (ManpowerGroup, *2015 Talent Shortage Survey*)

1 in 10

**employers leverage
untapped talent pools.**

no applicants at all. Yet, only 10 percent of these employers lever-age untapped talent pools (Figure 1.1).[14]

Faster hiring requires mass: You must build a critical mass of candidates to select from. Building mass requires tapping into overlooked pools of people.

Obstacle #2: Employing Interviewing Methods That Are Inaccurate and Slow

During conventional interviews, candidates are on their best behavior. As a result, interviews are often a poor barometer as to who will fail or succeed in a given role. Newer interview methods, such as behavioral interviewing, have only made the process lon-ger. Hundreds of books and articles have been written on how to beat behavioral interviews. These books and articles demonstrate simple methods for telling interviewers exactly what they want to hear.

Interviews cannot be a conceptual exercise. They must allow you to see proof then-and-there that a candidate can do the job and do it well.

Obstacle #3: Failing to Build and Maintain a Prospective Employee Pipeline

When a seat opens suddenly, the amount of activity it generates can feel overwhelming. Without an active talent pipeline, a frantic dance ensues. Managers have to handle extra work as the company tries to find suitable candidates. Days later, schedules have to be coordinated for phone screenings and interviews. Work piles up, good candidates take other jobs, and nerves fray.

Maintaining a pipeline of prospective employees eliminates the dance. When jobs open, there's no rush, panic, or chaos. Instead, you can hire from your overflowing pipeline.

The Need for Speed

In hiring, is there a need for speed? Only if the status quo dissatisfies you. That's why mindset matters so much. Moving into the fast lane requires a conscious decision and ongoing commitment. You've got to decide that, when it comes to hiring, from now on your organization will stand for speed.

You won't be navigating the world of fast hiring alone. I'll guide you through safely increasing the pace of every aspect of employee selection. I'll address how to eliminate the three obstacles that slow fast hiring. You'll discover how to implement a process that allows you to swiftly and accurately fill one role, several job titles, or all of your jobs in an instant.

What may surprise you is how familiar some of these ideas may seem. You're already living in a world getting quicker by the day. In our next chapter, we'll take a closer look at the principles that drive our fast-paced, on-demand economy and how they apply to fast and accurate hiring.

Action List for Chapter 1

To prepare your company for a faster approach to hiring, take the following steps.

Identify Negative Mindsets

Think about each of the people in your department or company involved in hiring. What negative mindsets do they bring to the task? Don't get angry with these people, and avoid trying to change their thinking. Just take note, knowing that these mindsets are where people are likely to resist or get stuck as you implement your faster hiring process.

Stay Informed, Not Immersed

It's prudent to stay informed about skills shortages, but dangerous to be immersed in tons of bad news and data. Daily work is hard enough without living under a cloud of gloom. There are credible sources that provide snapshots of talent shortages and hiring trends. Here are a few I rely upon:

Talent Shortage Survey from ManpowerGroup
This yearly survey of tens of thousands of hiring managers from dozens of countries provides current insights on the skills shortage.
www.manpowergroup.com/talentshortage

ASA Skills Gap Index
Published quarterly, The American Staffing Association's Skills Gap Index identifies the hardest-to-fill occupations in the United States.
www.americanstaffing.net/staffing-research-data/asa
-staffing-industry-data/asa-skills-gap-index

SHRM LINE: Leading Indicators of National Employment
The Society for Human Resource Management's LINE delivers monthly updates and an annual review of key hiring data, including employment expectations and recruiting difficulty.
www.shrm.org/hr-today/trends-and-forecasting/labor
-market-and-economic-data/pages/default.aspx

Spot Your Process Problems

Honestly appraise your complete hiring process. Where does it go well, slow down, or come to a halt? Which of the three hiring obstacles constitutes your organization's biggest downfall? How have negative mindsets contributed to the problem?

Knowing ahead of time which parts of your process are fast or slow is important. Your insights will help you keep what works and replace what doesn't with ideas from upcoming chapters.

Find the Early Adopters

Identify your company's early adopters. Early adopters are the people who are often first; they, for instance, wait in line for the new mobile device the day it's released. Their willingness, even desire, to be first makes them valuable partners for you. Share this book with them. By enrolling them now, you'll have ready-made collaborators to help you implement High Velocity Hiring.

The Talent Accelerator Process

Apply the Principles of the On-Demand Economy to Fill Jobs in an Instant

Once upon a time, if you wanted to watch a movie that had recently left the theaters, you had to take a trip to the video store first. After scanning the shelves and finding the right film, you'd pay a rental fee and head home, videocassette in hand. That entire process may have taken 20 minutes, and back then 20 minutes didn't seem like much. But, in today's on-demand world, when you can stream a movie in seconds, that same 20 minutes feels like an eternity. Breakneck speed is now the norm, and that speed keeps getting faster.

The need for speed has become a strategic requirement. Internet service providers continue one-upping each other by stomping on the download accelerator. Just a few years ago, my cable Internet service boasted a top speed of 40 megabytes. Today, I can web surf at seven times that speed.

Acquiring other services and products has also gotten quicker. Getting a massage while I'm traveling between speaking events used to require booking ahead. Now there's an app for that, which promises to have a licensed massage therapist at my door in an hour. I love the smell of books at my local bookstore, but it can be inconvenient to drive five miles when I can download a book in five seconds. Consider food, software, handyman services, stock trades, event tickets: The list of what we can buy, rent, or use now or minutes from now grows by the day.

In our on-demand world, we have come to expect that we should get what we want when we want it. That's the secret of fast, accurate hiring: Implementing a process that allows us to hire who we need, when we need them. It's about filling an open seat right now. Not weeks from now.

Our insatiable appetite for products and services on command has led to the creation of the on-demand economy. It becomes safe and easy to hire with speed when we apply the principles of the on-demand economy to employee recruitment. That's the essence of High Velocity Hiring—gaining the power to hire right now.

The Power of Right Now

Instant gratification drives the on-demand economy. The buying of products and services has been sped up by the Internet. However, the roots of on-demand can be found in a surprising place—automobile dealerships.

One of my summer jobs in the 1980s was working in a dealership, selling cars. I made a respectable commission. What was more valuable to me, though, was witnessing the power of immediacy. My job was to get people behind the wheel for a test drive. The firsthand experience of driving a car was more compelling than anything I could say. It was only natural after a test drive that a buyer would want to keep driving that car. Who can resist that new car smell?

To turn test drivers into same-day buyers, the dealer incorporated immediacy into the sales process. They'd let potentially creditworthy customers "buy" the car today. These customers would drive off the lot smiling, thinking the car was theirs. Actually, it wasn't. Not yet.

For decades, the fine print in automobile purchase agreements has granted dealers the power to cancel a purchase. Even after you sign the paperwork and hand them a down payment. Why? Because it takes a few days to verify your creditworthiness and locate financing for the contract's precise terms.

Do dealers end up cancelling deals? They do. At one particular dealership in Tampa Bay, Florida, it's not unusual for a couple of deals to be cancelled each month. A sales manager there told me this practice is worth the risk, because it allows them to satisfy everyone immediately. The buyer keeps driving the car and the dealership pulls the customer off the market. As he put it, "When they think their needs have been met, people stop looking. They drive their new car home, instead of shopping at other dealers."

That's the power of right now. Immediacy is engaging; delays are discouraging (Figure 2.1). When we get our needs met right now, we needn't keep looking. The longer that we have to wait, the more likely we are to consider other options.

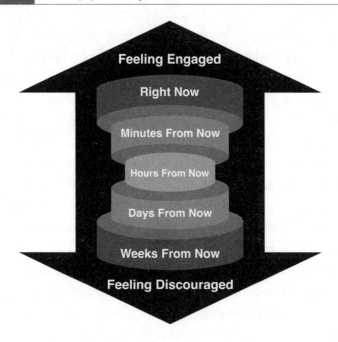

FIGURE 2.1   The Engagement Spectrum

A long hiring process is discouraging, prompting people to take matters into their own hands. Top talent will seek other opportunities when an employer fails to act quickly. Hiring managers will circumvent company policies when their jobs remain unfilled. Staffing agencies will shop candidates to other customers when buyers take too long to respond.

A fast on-demand approach to filling jobs leverages the power of now. When we're part of an efficient, forward-moving process, we feel in control. Feeling in control is satisfying and engaging, making it easier to trust the process and those who run the process.

Immediacy satisfies our human desire for instant gratification. Being able to buy almost anything from one source is convenient. Being able to buy it right now is gratifying. So much so that it's changed our expectations about the buying experience.

The Everything Store

Amazon.com has become a model for one-stop shopping. If your family is like mine, the Amazon name shows up on your credit card statement each month. Our list of purchases varies—books, batteries, allergy medicine, a coffee grinder, a kayak rack—but our reason for buying from Amazon is always the same. We trust the process. This process allows us to buy and receive products with relative ease and speed.

Amazon understands that selling a variety of products isn't enough to remain competitive. They recognize the importance of speed. In his book on the company, *The Everything Store*, Brad Stone shares details on how Amazon retains its competitive edge. This includes operating a group within the company called Competitive Intelligence. The group purchases large volumes of products from rivals and measures the quality and speed of their rivals' services. If Competitive Intelligence finds that a competitor is doing better than Amazon, the company addresses this emerging threat.[1]

Rather than just reacting to threats, Amazon has found ways to proactively increase value and speed. In 2004, the company began exploring a speedy shipping club for customers who needed products quickly.[2] The idea became Amazon Prime, a membership that includes free two-day shipping plus streaming videos, music, and eBooks. According to Stone, "The service turned customers into Amazon addicts who gorged on the almost instant gratification of having purchases reliably appear two days after they ordered them."[3]

In the on-demand economy fast keeps getting faster, and Amazon remains at the forefront of this acceleration. Amazon Dash allows customers to buy more than 100 products at the press of an in-home button. Customers order a branded button for a particular product, such as Tide or Doritos, place it in a visible spot, and sync it to the Amazon app. Then, when they run low on that item, they push the button, and it's on its way.[4]

Quick results are never an accident. Companies must mindfully consider the impact of acceleration on customers, suppliers, and their own organization. They plan a strategy that sustains or improves quality as speed of delivery increases. In executing the strategy, they carefully implement their plans, starting small and expanding with care. To maintain the benefits of their high-velocity delivery system, they work to keep their methods lean and efficient.

To get started, any organization wanting to achieve faster results—be it faster procurement of products, quicker access to services, or speeding up the filling of jobs—has to answer the following two questions:

- What can we do to increase speed without sacrificing quality and accuracy?

- How do we make this new speed sustainable?

Speed Versus Haste

When you answer the two previous questions about faster hiring, you aren't just thinking outside the box. "Sometimes, you have to blow up the box," said Obed Louissaint, vice president of people and culture for IBM Watson. That's exactly what Louissaint did when he joined the group's management team.

The goal of IBM Watson is to lead society into the next era of computing, creating new tools that help people do what they couldn't do before. To achieve this, Louissaint and his recruiting team had to ensure they had qualified people, exactly when they were needed—without ever hiring in haste.

"There's a big difference between speed and haste," said Louissaint. "Haste has no place in employee selection. Rushed decisions often lead to poor choices. These mistakes result from an ineffective approach that wasn't built to deliver fast and accurate hires. Speed is different. It is simply part of a well-planned process for achieving great results quickly."

Rather than make hasty hiring decisions based on whim, Louissaint has formally baked speed into IBM Watson's process for talent acquisition. "The operative words are plan and process," he says. "Fast and accurate hiring isn't a fluke. It happens because leaders plan for it, implement a process to achieve it, and hold people accountable to following the plan."

Paradoxically, hiring quickly can't be done in haste. Haste causes harm to companies and careers. Organizations need a streamlined employee selection process that allows them to make intelligent decisions without cutting corners or compromising values.

Seven principles underlie the on-demand economy. Applying these principles allows companies to deliver their products and services with speed, not haste. When applied to hiring, these same principles allow organizations to design a recruitment process that is fast, accurate, and efficient.

The Seven Principles of an On-Demand System

Applied in order, the following seven principles create the framework for increasing speed without sacrificing quality (Figure 2.2).

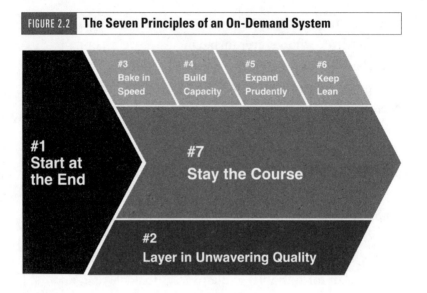

FIGURE 2.2   The Seven Principles of an On-Demand System

#3 Bake in Speed

#4 Build Capacity

#5 Expand Prudently

#6 Keep Lean

#1 Start at the End

#7 Stay the Course

#2 Layer in Unwavering Quality

Principle #1: Start at the End

Jeff Bezos, founder and CEO of Amazon.com, didn't just wake up one day and decide to start selling memberships for Prime. The idea was suggested by Amazon engineer Charlie Ward.[5] He recognized that not all Amazon customers are price conscious; some have needs that are time-sensitive. His recommendation for a speedy shipping club resulted from his awareness that the company could better meet the needs of customers who wanted expedited shipping. To make this idea work, Amazon had to identify and overcome pitfalls and then sell the positive impacts of this new service.

Starting at the end allows organizations to determine why there is a need for faster results and the impacts, positive and negative, this will create. Specifying the desired outcome and its positive impacts makes it a tangible goal, one whose benefits can be easily communicated. Taking time up front to identify potential pitfalls allows leaders to design a process that addresses those issues.

Deciding to hire faster starts at the end. Your company will need to decide whether it wants to fill one, several, or many jobs in an instant. That decision will have positive impacts that help you engage your colleagues, and possible pitfalls that will require attention. That's why this principle is the first and most important. It will guide every other decision you make.

Principle #2: Layer in Unwavering Quality

My experiences with taxis has been mixed. Dirty cabs, smelly drivers, and frightful driving turned some cab rides into an adventure. Not so with Uber. Clean cars and drivers who got me to my destinations with care have made me a repeat customer. A friend who works for Uber explained that drivers agree to maintain a high standard of professional service. When a customer complains, the company follows up to address the issue, terminating relationships when those issues persist.

Maintaining quality as speed increases has to be an immutable standard. How? It's part of the plan. Methods are included in the process that ensure and measure quality, including steps for rectifying any problems that arise. Speed and quality become interdependent rather than mutually exclusive.

Speed can never supplant quality when hiring. The two must go hand-in-hand. An accelerated process has to improve quality, ensuring that your company can quickly make smart choices versus hires you later regret.

Principle #3: Bake in Speed

Companies who deliver on-demand prepare to be fast. Take Jimmy John's for example. Late one night, I was the sole customer dining in at a Jimmy John's outside of Milwaukee. I watched staff members carefully weighing meats and cheeses, stacking them between sheets of deli paper. Bins were filled with sandwich toppings, bread was set out at prep stations, and bags and cups were stacked in their appropriate spots. This is why Jimmy John's can offer freaky fast delivery. At the end of each day, they prepare to be fast tomorrow.

A faster process has speed baked in. This includes a streamlined system for achieving the end result, including methods that address those previously identified pitfalls. Simplicity is also baked in to assure sustainability and ease of communicating the process.

Hiring is more complex than building a sandwich. However, it's become an overly complicated, slow process with too many steps and too much effort. Streamlining how hiring is done requires that you do less labor-intensive work that achieves better hires quickly.

Principle #4: Build Capacity

The initial introduction of Amazon Dash was by invitation only. Controlling the number of customers who accessed this new service allowed the company to mindfully roll out, test, and tweak the program. A few months later, it was made available to the general public for a limited number of products, the next phase of mindful expansion. The rollout expanded from there to include Dash buttons for other products.

Building capacity starts with preparation, coordinating plans for implementation with competing demands and the availability of time and resources. The initial rollout is done with care, without unnecessarily overtaxing people or systems. Capacity is increased prudently, allowing for adjustments and changes to the process, as necessary, to maintain quality and speed.

Implementing a faster hiring system will require that you have the same degree of thoughtfulness. Your timelines and deadlines should be considered carefully. You'll need to allocate adequate time and resources without undermining other initiatives. Like many organizations, you may choose to start with one position in one department, leveraging positive results as a catalyst to incrementally increase capacity.

Principle #5: Expand Prudently

Netflix has become an award-winning producer of original series like *House of Cards* and *Orange Is the New Black*, an impressive result for a movie rental company. The evolution from delivering DVDs by mail to a streaming movie service to an Internet television network exemplifies prudent expansion. The leaders of Netflix had to plan, execute, and troubleshoot their growth carefully while always keeping the end in mind: Providing members with the ability to watch as much programming as they want, anytime, anywhere.[6]

Maintaining fulfillment capabilities beyond market demand is a requirement for prudent expansion. Immediacy is always at the heart of being on-demand. The end-goal is always top of mind, guiding efforts and focusing ambitions. Plans are constantly compared to desired results; what contributes to the goal is maintained and what detracts from the goal is removed.

Fast and accurate hiring requires vigilance: Your process should be expanded prudently and never be pushed to deliver beyond its capabilities. Your colleagues must be able to trust the process.

Principle #6: Keep Lean

Surprise projects with short deadlines are common in today's world of work. For instance, my colleague Sam recently needed a press release, a task he had never undertaken before. He turned to his favorite "get it done quick" resource—Upwork. This on-demand provider of freelancers boosts 12 million workers, matching them to projects like Sam's. It took him just a few minutes to post his need by answering a handful of questions and checking a few boxes. Later that day, 12 freelancers had applied, one of whom Sam selected for the job.

Managing a platform of millions of people who do $1 billion in work for five million customers is no small task.[7] Upwork has had to keep lean as it's grown big, avoiding wasted time or effort. Their team has to serve customers, implement new ideas, and fix problems while maintaining a speedy and accurate matchmaking service.

Keeping an on-demand system lean is essential in meeting the shifting demands of customers. Technology must reduce effort. Time has to be spent wisely. Resources need to be conserved. Maintaining the system requires constant attention, with focus on finding and eliminating wasted time, resources, and effort. Fast delivery of products to people or people for jobs only happens when your lean and efficient system can make that happen.

Principle #7: Stay the Course

For an on-demand plan to work, that plan needs to be followed. Sometimes, doing so is easier said than done. After all, the economy ebbs and flows, markets change, and employees come and go. There's a lot to attend to, and some of it is unpredictable.

All of the companies highlighted in these principles, however, have achieved success because they've stayed the course. They may adjust plans or improve their process, yet they know that consistent action is a requirement for delivering quality products and services with speed and accuracy.

Fast hiring isn't a one-time event; it's a commitment to a process. Your organization will need to plan, implement, and sustain a faster hiring process, and then stay the course. This will also require consistent execution and continuous improvement, keeping the endgame—being able to hire top talent in an instant—always top of mind.

The Intimacy of a Faster Process

Not everyone immediately embraces the idea of applying the principles of the on-demand economy to hiring. At a meeting of the leadership team of a health insurance company, one leader, Paul, thought the idea was "repulsive." As we discussed how to plan a faster recruiting process using the seven principles, Paul started making passive-aggressive comments. After he said, "What's next? We're going to replace our employees with robots, like in that Will Smith movie," I knew our discussion wasn't addressing all of his concerns. I asked Paul to explain.

"People aren't products," he said angrily. "I can't believe we're even discussing such a dehumanizing approach. Picking the right people takes time. Interviews, even if they last all day, are a good investment of our time. We must make sure we're picking the best people. Besides, good candidates won't want to be rushed through the process. I'm finding this whole conversation repulsive. I'm sure my team will feel the same way."

Instead of trying to convince Paul to change his mind, I decided to let him change it himself (which is one of the principles you'll learn about later in the book). I said, "Paul, thanks for your honesty. I bet you're not the only one with concerns about a faster approach." Two other leaders nodded their heads in agreement. "What would you need to determine if this could work for the company?" Paul thoughtfully paused before responding, "I'd need to see proof. Absolute proof that this will work for us."

That led to a conversation about rolling out a faster hiring process on a limited basis to start. Two leaders, who didn't share Paul's concerns, agreed to test the process. Choosing a job common to both of their departments, we applied the seven principles, designing a plan and timeline that could be implemented without interrupting day-to-day business. Two other leaders, including Paul, were designated as auditors, outside observers who would monitor and document the pros and cons as the process was rolled out.

(continued)

I met again with the leadership team after the beginning of the rollout. The two managers testing the process gave updates, sharing mostly positive news. They had made a few missteps along the way; however, both were upbeat. Both had filled two open jobs and lined up several additional candidates in their pipelines as potential future hires.

During their updates, I watched Paul out of the corner of my eye. He spent the entire time looking down at his notes. He appeared angry, even angrier than when he shared his concerns in our first meeting. I learned why when it was Paul's turn to share pros and cons as an auditor of the test. "I hate being wrong," he said. "But, there it is. I was flat out wrong. There was nothing dehumanizing about a faster approach. If anything, it enabled interviewers to focus on people, not process. This shorter, simpler process allowed them to get to know each other better. Our new hires told me they loved our efficient process, and that it was a factor in choosing to work here."

When hiring, speed and accuracy are not mutually exclusive. Nor are speed and intimacy. A well-designed, well-executed hiring process allows people to be fully present and have conversations that matter. These interactions build trust, as candidates learn they are dealing with confident professionals, and hiring managers discover which candidates are ready to make a job change. This trust becomes the foundation for the employment relationship, one built on a professionally intimate hiring experience.

The Principles in Action

Filling 300 jobs can be a challenge. Filling 300 jobs when you can guarantee only a few months' work would make it much harder. Doing so in five weeks could seem impossible.

Eric Houwen was faced with this task in 2015. As the recruitment manager for CAK, Houwen's team was responsible for recruiting talent for open jobs. CAK, a government-related organization, plays a central role in Holland's complicated healthcare system. The organization collects and analyzes data from thousands of institutions and agencies, calculates the associated healthcare charges, and bills and collects payments from consumers.

In January 2015, a new set of regulations altered the amount consumers had to pay, and CAK knew their call center would be bombarded by queries from people questioning their bills. In preparation for these calls, CAK realized they'd need to hire 300 additional call center employees. These employees had to be in place by the time consumers received their next bill, just weeks away.

"Our recruiting team would typically work on 80 jobs a month," said Houwen. "Because of this project, our workload increased nearly 500 percent overnight." Houwen's job was made even harder by a number of factors. "The majority of our recruiting team dealing with this project was new to CAK. Plus, we were recruiting in a new region as well. In trying to get people interested in the job, we could promise them only a few months of full-time employment. This project was thrilling and daunting."

The short timeline didn't lessen the demand for making quality hires. "There were no concessions to be made," said Houwen. "This initiative was too important to settle for subpar talent. New hires would need excellent communication skills and had to be able to ramp up quickly. We had to find a way to take our existing vetting process and somehow squeeze it into the amount of time we were granted."

With the end-goal and timeline set, Houwen and his team had to develop a faster approach. They implemented an on-demand process that allowed them to review hundreds of candidates a day. These candidates were initially sourced from numerous resources, including job boards and referrals. To keep the process fast and lean, they quickly narrowed these resources to those that were generating the best candidates. Interviews were also quick and efficient; recruiters were able to swiftly assess who fit their rigorous standards and who did not. The recruiting team rapidly gained momentum, allowing them to build and expand capacity quickly.

Did they succeed in hiring and onboarding 300 call center agents in five weeks? Yes, and feedback about the quality of these hires was excellent. "The first week our call center managed 36,000 calls," said Houwen. "We couldn't have done that without adding those extra agents."

Houwen has moved on to a new role, but this experience left an indelible impression. "That kind of an assignment is why we became recruiters. It was a chance to make a real difference. And we did. We built an effective on-demand hiring system in a matter of weeks. The quality of those employees ended up being as good, or even a little better in some cases, than hires we had made before. I know that faster hiring isn't just possible. We've proven it works."[8]

Push-Button Hiring

When a job opens, wouldn't it be nice if you had a button, like Amazon's Dash, which once pushed would fill your job in an instant? There may not be a button, but there's a process—one that incorporates all seven principles of an on-demand system. It's called the Talent Accelerator Process (TAP) (Figure 2.3).

TAP is the engine that propels High Velocity Hiring. By design, it allows your company to fill one job or many roles in

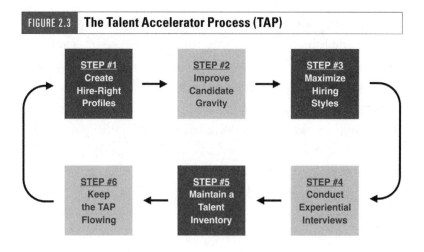

FIGURE 2.3 The Talent Accelerator Process (TAP)

an instant. Quality and speed are incorporated into every step, ensuring you can quickly and accurately select the best people. TAP lets you build capacity at your pace and expand its use as you see fit. While the process is inherently lean, methods are provided to help you keep it fast and efficient. Staying the course simply requires maintaining a healthy flow of quality candidates. TAP is the practical application of the new way of hiring: Actively cultivating top talent and then waiting for the right job to open.

The operative word in High Velocity Hiring is flow. The Talent Accelerator Process enriches the flow of candidates by drawing in more people with the correct qualifications. Harnessing this flow leverages human perception during interviews, providing proof that someone is, or is not, the correct fit. Creating a pool of ready-to-hire, prospective employees sustains the flow, enabling your company to hire on-demand. The next six chapters will walk you through each step of TAP, providing all of the details you need to engage in High Velocity Hiring.

Starting at the end is the most important of the principles of an on-demand system. That's why our next chapter focuses on hiring profiles. You must know who is a good fit if you're going to find and select the right people. Unfortunately, many leaders avoid creating or using hiring profiles, finding them time-consuming to create. Not so with Hire-Right Profiles. By the end of the next chapter, you'll be ready to write your first one in 20 minutes or less.

Action List for Chapter 2

The following steps will help you plan your implementation of the Talent Accelerator Process.

Address Fears of Fast Hiring

Now's a good time to share your interest in speeding up your hiring process. As you do, you may find resistance, even fear, among people in your company. This is normal. Going faster can seem unsafe, even dangerous. Take, for instance, a new roller coaster at an amusement park—one that sets a new record for speed. Some people need to watch others safely riding it first before they'll give it a try.

Having a discussion about the on-demand economy may help your colleagues see the benefits and safety of speed. For example, you could ask people to make a list of products and services that are available now on-demand. These could include banking, office supplies, software, travel, and food. Discuss how long it used to take to acquire or use each one. Ask for opinions on how companies were able to speed up their processes without sacrificing quality. Review how those process ideas could be used at your company to create an on-demand system for hiring.

Distinguish Between Speed and Haste

Comparing speed and haste can also help people overcome their concerns about fast hiring. One way to do this is by conducting a brainstorming session on the differences between speed and haste, using two columns to compare the two (Table 2.1).

TABLE 2.1	Speed Versus Haste

SPEED	HASTE
Choosing more expensive recruiting resources that quickly provide a handful of good candidates.	Choosing less expensive recruiting resources that quickly provide hundreds of candidates, a few of which may be good.
Completing reference checks during face-to-face interviews, allowing an offer to be made promptly thereafter.	Skipping reference checks after several failed attempts to reach people after face-to-face interviews.
Immediately offering the job to a candidate who meets all of the requirements.	Immediately offering the job to a candidate who meets most, but not all, of the requirements.

Make Important Decisions Now

Several important decisions need to be made before you implement the Talent Accelerator Process (TAP). To do so, answer the following questions:

1. Will you use TAP to fill one, several, or many jobs in an instant?

   It may be tempting to respond "several" or "many." However, that answer may not be what your company needs. The impact of a job remaining unfilled is greater for some roles than others. Before answering this question, it's useful to group jobs into three categories:

a) **Core Roles:** An open seat creates an immediate and significant negative impact. The nature or amount of work in this role makes it hard to delegate. Filling the job, because of market demand, tends to be difficult.

b) **Essential Roles:** A job opening has a negative impact, but is less severe than a core role. The nature or amount of work isn't as hard to delegate, but is still vital to the company. Filling an essential role is challenging, but tends to take no more than a few weeks.

c) **Supportive Roles:** Supportive jobs are important; however, openings for these roles have less impact when compared to core and essential jobs. Work is easier to delegate or cover while a replacement is found. Finding qualified candidates to interview for these roles usually takes a matter of days.

Once you categorize your jobs, you'll have a clearer picture of how to prioritize which ones you'll initially fill using TAP.

2. Which aspects of our hiring process already provide us with a quick, high-quality result?

The action list for Chapter 1 included identifying which parts of your hiring process are fast or slow. Review that list, adding any specific current methods you may have missed that are already lean and effective. As you incorporate TAP, you'll have the opportunity to incorporate those into the process.

3. Are there scheduling conflicts or competing demands in the coming months?

   Identify important dates and initiatives over the next three to six months. As you plan your implementation of TAP, you'll want to carefully manage your time and resources to avoid unnecessarily overtaxing people and systems.

Step #1—
Create Hire-Right
Profiles

Design Blueprints Detailing
Who's Right for a Job

Dating and interviewing have a lot in common. Both are about getting to know one another better and can lead to a long-term relationship. This courtship can become something very special—a fulfilling and nurturing partnership that meets the needs of all involved.

For decades, I've believed that healthy dating was a great metaphor for filling jobs. What I didn't expect was that the metaphor would be put to the test in my personal life after my first marriage ended in 2007. This marriage taught me a lot about the importance of compatibility. I knew I wanted to put this knowledge to use when I was ready to date again. Being completely honest with myself, I acknowledged I had never experienced healthy dating. Because of this, I was convinced that I lacked the experience to pick the right women to date.

I was wrong or at least forgetful. I had proven methods for fast and accurate hiring, so I simply needed to adapt those methods to dating. Selecting appropriate people to interview or date is where it all begins. Applying my Hire-Right Profile, a process for creating a blueprint for who is the best fit for a job, made sense as the place to start.

I sat down with my laptop and filled in a "Dating-Right Profile," my new name for this romantic version of my hiring system. Like a Hire-Right Profile, it had four quadrants. Each quadrant detailed important criteria for potential dating partners: Dealmakers (my must haves), Dealbreakers (my must not haves), Boosts (additional positive attributes that would be nice to have), and Blocks (negative attributes that I preferred not be present).

I started by listing my Dealmakers. I thought through and noted the attributes of people with whom I was compatible in personal and professional situations. These attributes included a good sense of humor, consistent follow-through, healthy work–life balance, and the ability to be emotionally present.

Thinking about challenging relationships, unhealthy friendships, and toxic interactions at work helped me create my Dealbreakers. I pondered those associations, identifying the underlying traits that made them difficult. My list of Dealbreakers included a drama-filled life, a victim mentality, and manipulative behavior.

I paused for a moment, reviewing what I'd come up with so far. I had noted a dozen Dealmakers and about the same number of Dealbreakers. I was forming a clear picture of who was and who was not a fit. That allowed for some daydreaming about my

Boosts and Blocks. I pictured travel and cooking meals with a significant other, adding these to my list of Boosts. Someone who lived out of town or traveled a lot for work made my list of Blocks.

In 20 minutes, I was done. I knew exactly who I was looking for. As I began to date, I found it surprisingly easy to identify women who matched my needs and wants. Each person I met was compared to my Dating-Right Profile. As Dealmakers showed up, I'd check those off and continue. If a Dealbreaker appeared, I'd kindly end our interactions.

My greatest concern in using my hiring profile for romantic purposes was that it would turn dating into a cold, dispassionate exercise. That was not the case. My Dating-Right Profile took away much of the pressure of picking potential matches and getting dating right. I knew that I could show up and just be me, having enjoyable encounters with women who may or may not be a fit for a relationship. My dating profile helped me make logical choices about something that can often feel illogical and emotionally overwhelming.

Dating was enjoyable, at times stress free. Did it go flawlessly? No. A few dates were awkward, especially with several women who had misrepresented themselves. The upside was that those awkward dates helped me fine-tune my Dating-Right Profile. The more I used it, the better I got at choosing women to ask out. I had many lovely first dates, with a few moving beyond that point. However, each of those ended after a Dealbreaker appeared, or it become clear that a Dealmaker was missing. Until I met Holly.

My first date with Holly was supposed to last an hour. Instead, we talked for three, after which I ended up checking off a number of Dealmakers. A second date led to a third and then a fourth and then I stopped counting. It was crystal clear that a relationship with Holly had real potential. Over the following months, I realized I had found someone with every one of my Dealmakers and none of those show-stopping Dealbreakers. Holly also had a number of those bonus traits listed in my Boosts and none of the Blocks. I was falling head over heels in love.

It was easy to fall in love with Holly. Not only because of the caliber of person she was, but because I knew that I was honoring my needs. It was safe to be present and build a relationship. We were married in New York City's Central Park after a three-year courtship. It even rained for a few minutes during the ceremony, which, supposedly, brings good luck. However, I know that luck had nothing to do with the wonderful marriage I have today. It exists because I planned for it, selected a good match, and fell in love. My romantic version of the Hire-Right Profile allowed me to make logical choices rather than allowing my decision making to be ruled by emotion.

The Emotional Element of Hiring

Emotions, even those that are unpleasant, are an important part of being human. The problem with emotions experienced during hiring is their inherent ability to compromise sound decision making. We select the wrong people for the wrong reasons when our feelings get in the way.

In a conversation about the impact of emotions on hiring, human resources veteran Pam O'Connor acknowledged how problematic emotionality can be when trying to select someone for a job. "I've worked with lots of smart leaders in the profit and not-for-profit sectors," she said. "Unfortunately, I witnessed many of them make emotional hiring decisions that turned out poorly. From my experience, I believe that emotions are a top factor for why good candidates become bad hires."

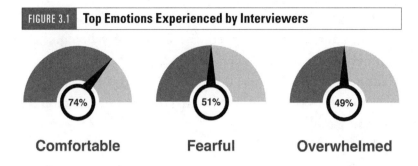

FIGURE 3.1 | **Top Emotions Experienced by Interviewers**

74%

Comfortable

51%

Fearful

49%

Overwhelmed

During her tenure as an HR executive in top organizations including retailer Wet Seal, healthcare firm Baxter, and global charity Catholic Relief Services, O'Connor participated in thousands of interviews. She saw a direct correlation between emotionality and effective selection. "When hiring managers are emotionally triggered during the interview process," said O'Connor, "the more likely their hires will leave or be terminated prematurely."

O'Connor's experience of the impacts of emotions on hiring parallels my own. In reviewing 410 failed hires (defined as employment lasting less than six months), 92 percent of the managers who had hired those individuals experienced emotions that they believe had a negative impact during their interviews (Figure 3.1). For example, feeling overwhelmed at having to manage the additional workload of an open job while also conducting interviews was a common emotion. Fearfulness over losing a potentially good candidate to a competitor was reported by more than half the managers. The most frequently mentioned emotion was being comfortable with the individual being interviewed. In exploring this particular feeling, managers agreed that feeling comfortable with a candidate made it easier to overlook required or desired traits that were missing.

In an analysis of 35 years of research on emotions and decision making, Harvard experimental social psychologist Dr. Jennifer Lerner found that emotions can have an unconscious and undesirable impact on decisions.[1] Emotions that are unrelated to a decision can skew thinking, causing people to make poor choices.[2]

A feeling of being comfortable with a candidate, for example, is a distraction. It interferes when managers are determining if a candidate has all of the necessary traits to perform well in a job. Being comfortable with a potential hire may be desirable, but it can unintentionally undermine making a hiring decision based upon factual evidence. The same is true of fearfulness and being overwhelmed. Feeling fearful about losing a good candidate to a competitor does not mean she is the correct fit for the job. Feeling overwhelmed about additional responsibilities, such as interviews and an increased workload, can easily distract a hiring manager from making a sound choice.

The emotion inherent in hiring is why active use of hiring profiles is important. Just as my dating version of the Hire-Right Profile allowed me to make smart decisions in emotionally charged situations, the same kind of objectivity is gained from having a job candidate blueprint.

Unfortunately, many of the companies who have engaged me to consult with them since 1999 had hiring profiles that were inaccurate or simply not followed during the selection process. Instead of countering distracting emotions experienced during and after interviews, leaders in these companies ended up relying on "gut" feelings.

Feelings are not facts. Emotions, left unchecked, can become false evidence that candidates fit roles they do not. Hire-Right Profiles allow you to swiftly make objective decisions based on factual evidence.

The Hire-Right Profile

You can create a Hire-Right Profile in under 20 minutes. The setup is simple and the format familiar—a four-quadrant table (Figure 3.2).

Quadrant #1 (upper left)—Dealmakers

Dealmakers are required attributes. Candidates must have every attribute in this quadrant to be considered for hire.

Quadrant #2 (upper right)—Dealbreakers

Dealbreakers are knockout factors. Having any of these Dealbreakers eliminates a candidate from contention.

FIGURE 3.2   **The Hire-Right Profile**

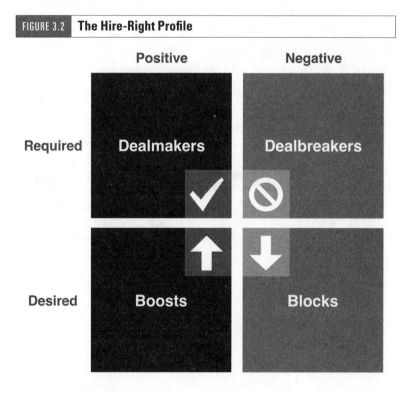

Quadrant #3 (lower left)—Boosts

Boosts are desirable attributes. While not a requirement to be hired, the more Boosts someone has the more likely he will be an exceptional hire.

Quadrant #4 (lower right)—Blocks

Blocks are undesirable traits. While having any of these does not preclude hiring a candidate, each one that is present increases the likelihood that employment will end in disappointment or failure.

TABLE 3.1	Sample Hire-Right Profile: Sales Role

DEALMAKERS	DEALBREAKERS
• Healthy overachiever, demonstrated by consistently exceeding expectations	• Complains daily about the latest difficulty or injustice
• Money-motivated, especially in needing to earn beyond base compensation	• Constantly late to meetings or appointments
• Follows directions	• Misses deadlines regularly
• Communicates effectively in person and over the telephone	• People-pleaser personality, showing too much concern about what others think
• Collaborative curiosity	• Lack of self-discipline
• Fearless tenacity	• Sells price instead of value
• Tempered impatience	• Speaks more than listens

BOOSTS	BLOCKS
• Professional fund-raising experience, demonstrating fearlessness in asking for money	• Master's degree in an analytical area
• Previous business-to-business sales experience	• Previous focus on RFP business versus building exclusive business arrangements
• Bachelor's degree or higher	• Long tenure in selling commodity products or services
• Experience building and maintaining a social network of at least 2,000 people	• Unable to travel at a moment's notice
• Strong written communication skills, especially in writing emails that are concise and complete	

A well-thought-out Hire-Right Profile contains enough detail to clearly differentiate who fits a job, and who does not. Every role has its own unique Hire-Right Profile. When a role has varying levels, each level of that role has its own version. For instance, in comparing the sample Hire-Right Profile in Table 3.1 to Table 3.2,

TABLE 3.2	Sample Hire-Right Profile: Senior Sales Role

DEALMAKERS	DEALBREAKERS
• Healthy overachiever, demonstrated by consistently exceeding expectations	• Complains daily about the latest difficulty or injustice
• Money-motivated, especially in needing to earn beyond base compensation	• Constantly late to meetings or appointments
• Follows directions	• Regularly misses deadlines
• Communicates effectively in person and over the telephone	• People-pleaser personality, showing too much concern about what others think
• Collaborative curiosity	• Lack of self-discipline
• Fearless tenacity	• Sells price instead of value
• Tempered impatience	• Speaks more than listens
• **Experience in successfully expanding a local territory into new geographic areas**	
• **Successfully serving as a mentor for at least three salespeople, with each mentee exceeding production expectations**	

BOOSTS	BLOCKS
• Professional fund-raising experience, demonstrating fearlessness in asking for money	• Master's degree in an analytical area
	• Previous focus on RFP business versus building exclusive business arrangements
• Previous business-to-business sales experience	• Long tenure in selling commodity products or services
• Bachelor's degree or higher	• Unable to travel at a moment's notice
• Experience building and maintaining a social network of at least 2,000 people	
• Strong written communication skills, especially in writing emails that are concise and complete	

two additional criteria were added to the blueprint for the senior-level version of the job.

What you're likely to appreciate most about Hire-Right Profiles is the detail. Each profile contains all the information you'll need for choosing the right person. Every requirement and knockout factor, along with pluses and minuses, can be found in one spot. Instead of worrying about missing an important attribute, everyone involved in recruiting or interviewing candidates follows the blueprint.

Adding Your Hiring Criteria

Whether you've interviewed hundreds or a handful of people, those experiences will shape your Hire-Right Profiles. Also, your observations of past and current employees who have succeeded and failed in the role will provide valuable details as to what makes or breaks a good hire. The following questions will uncover those details.

Question #1—Dealmakers

What are the common assets of employees who have succeeded in the job? These assets include an employee's skills, experiences, values, education, helpful behaviors, and personality features.

As you consider potential Dealmakers, think about all of the assets of people, including past and current employees, who have succeeded in the role. Which skills and previous work experiences do they have in common? When comparing their personal values, behaviors, and personality features, which ones were integral to their success in the role and compatibility with your culture? How did their education impact their ability to perform well in the job?

Look for patterns of assets. Assets common among successful hires are Dealmakers. Assets appearing in only a few people are Boosts.

Question #2—Dealbreakers

What are the common deficits of employees who have not succeeded in the job? These deficits include unhelpful behaviors, counterproductive actions, conflicting values, and negative personality features.

Using the same process you used for Dealmakers, look for patterns among the deficits of people who failed, or who are currently failing, to meet expectations. Each deficit that shows up consistently is a Dealbreaker; deficits that appear in only a few individuals are added to the quadrant of Blocks.

Question #3—Boosts

In addition to Dealmakers, what other assets were exhibited by top performers?

The more Boosts a candidate has, the more likely she will consistently perform well in the role. You'll uncover some of these answers in the first question about Dealmakers.

An in-depth review of top performers in the job will uncover additional Boosts. Think about what was truly unique about each individual who did exceptionally well. Which skills did they have that others did not? What experience did they bring to the company that was different? What differentiated the personalities and behaviors of these top performers from everyone else? Every additional detail about these noteworthy employees becomes part of the list of Boosts in the lower left quadrant.

Question #4—Blocks

In addition to Dealbreakers, what other deficits were exhibited by employees who were mediocre performers?

Blocks are attributes that, individually, don't typically cause someone to fail. However, the more Blocks someone accrues, the greater the chance he will struggle. Even when a candidate has every Dealmaker and none of the Dealbreakers, Blocks can undermine assets.

Carefully review past and current employees whose job performance was disappointing. You're looking for hires whose tenures were nothing spectacularly good or bad. What were their negative attributes? List each attribute that is not already noted as a Dealbreaker in your Blocks.

Ask your colleagues, such as your boss and employees that report to you, to independently answer these same questions. Watch for patterns among the details as you compare their input. Traits that appear three or more times in your collective answers to each question should always be included in the correct section of a completed profile.

Your HR or talent acquisition department can be a helpful resource when creating Hire-Right Profiles. Colleagues in those departments who have been closely involved with your team should be asked to answer the four questions. Also, many HR departments maintain files of performance reviews of past and current employees. These should be perused as well, looking for assets and deficits for inclusion in the Hire-Right Profile.

Existing Hire-Right Profiles can be used as templates for new jobs in the same department. Traits are often transferable for a new role, especially those that relate to values, helpful behaviors, and personality. Additional skills, experiences, and education can be identified using a variety of different resources, including:

- Friendly competitors who are open to an exchange of ideas.

- Job postings for similar roles at other companies; these can be found on company websites and on job boards.

- Websites that provide lists of job descriptions; examples include:
  www.job-descriptions.org
  hiring.monster.com/hr/hr-best-practices/recruiting-hiring
  -advice/job-descriptions/sample-job-descriptions.aspx

- Membership in an HR, staffing, or employment-related association may include access to job description templates. For instance, SHRM provides its members with dozens of sample job descriptions on their website.

- Profiles on LinkedIn, especially details that people list about their job experience and skills.

When you create and use Hire-Right Profiles for each role in your company, you gain significant advantages over people who hire by gut alone. Employee selection is done subjectively, based on accurate criteria. Your emotions, rather than running the show, are balanced with facts and logic. Instincts and gut feelings inform sound decision making versus being the primary selection method.

More important, faith in the process, versus fear of making a bad choice, allows you to make fast and accurate hiring decisions. Instead of losing talented people to more nimble competitors, Hire-Right Profiles allow you to secure top talent and fill open seats in an instant.

Recommended Assets

No two companies are exactly alike, even when they're in the same industry. Job titles vary, as do the skill requirements and interpersonal traits that best fit each organization's culture. As a result, no two Hire-Right Profiles end up exactly alike, even when comparing similar roles at different companies.

There are, however, role-specific assets that often get overlooked, and should appear in almost any company's Hire-Right Profiles. Here are three examples of such roles and their matching assets:

Role: Executive Leadership

Asset: Helicopter Leadership Skills
Executives who have successfully maneuvered between a 30,000-foot understanding of the marketplace, a 15,000-foot strategic viewpoint, and a ground-level perspective of the daily operations of their company are said to be "helicopter leaders." They make better decisions. Helicopter leadership allows them to combine a visionary outlook with current realities to create smart strategies.

Asset: Professional Humility
Humble executives acknowledge their own limitations, rather than being driven by an unhealthy ego. Their self-awareness and healthy self-confidence allow them to surround themselves with people who have strengths and abilities they themselves lack.

Asset: Inventor Mindset
Executives with an inventor mindset view failures as opportunities. They encourage those around them to leverage mistakes as a chance to improve capabilities and deepen relationships.

Role: Sales

Asset: Collaborative Curiosity
Curious salespeople ask better questions. They get to know their buyers and their needs, taking time to uncover detailed information. This creates lasting relationships built on trust and understanding.

(continued)

Asset: Fearless Tenacity

Over 80 percent of deals close after the fifth contact with a prospect. Fearlessly tenacious salespeople are the ones who keep showing up, knowing that every "no" moves them that much closer to the next buyer who will say "yes."

Asset: Tempered Impatience

Impatience in sales professionals can be a virtue, but only if it's tempered with a focus on the greater good. Salespeople with tempered impatience are motivated to help customers improve their circumstances as soon as possible. They're driven to build and maintain mutually beneficial relationships.

Role: Customer Service

Asset: Boundary-Setter

Problem resolution is vital to excellent customer service, as long as it doesn't go too far. People who have a proven track record for setting boundaries in a kind and compassionate manner deliver service that's respected and remembered.

Asset: Collaborative Compromise

When customers require help, savvy customer service pros avoid trying to resolve the situation on their own. Instead, they collaborate with customers, remembering that two heads are better than one.

Asset: Outcome-Achiever

The world is filled with people who care too much about how they're seen by others. Such people-pleasers focus on their own likability. Outcome-achievers strive to create a positive outcome for all parties, knowing that compromise is more potent than popularity.

Your Hire-Right Profiles must reflect your organization's values, needs, and culture in order to be useful. When considering these recommended traits for your roles, review each one carefully, making sure they fit your specific needs and culture.

In Appendix B, you'll find additional recommended assets for other job categories.

Trust the Process

When we began working together, Sharon Strauss was no stranger to using hiring profiles. Strauss is vice president of client services at Vitamin T, a global talent agency that serves creative digital professionals. She came to me, wanting to improve Vitamin T's hiring process for internal staff. "Our biggest challenge, hands down, was getting our staff away from hiring with their gut," she said. "If they really liked someone, they wanted to hire that person, even if there were indicators that she was not the best fit."

It took a few minutes over the phone to walk Strauss through the structure of the Hire-Right Profile. The familiarity of a four-quadrant table and the straightforward labels for each quadrant make it simple to share this with anyone, anywhere. After outlining the structure for her, Strauss took it from there. She filled in each section and, along the way, discovered several key insights. "Identifying Dealmakers was relatively easy. Once I started listing those, it was hard to stop. They flowed from my head to my hand to the paper. When I moved on to Dealbreakers, I initially found myself listing the opposites of my Dealmakers. That's why using the four questions to guide the process was important. As I refocused on the deficits of employees who had not succeeded in the job, identifying Dealbreakers became easier."

The simple design of these candidate blueprints has allowed Vitamin T to implement a standardized hiring tool that can be used companywide. In rolling out Hire-Right Profiles, Strauss quickly learned how the tool would make their good selection methods better. "I realized we'd been on track with most of our selection criteria," she said. "The problem was we often gave into gut feelings. We can now call each other out when we're compromising, and hold one another accountable to sticking to the plan and trusting the process."

Strauss' advice to first-time Hire-Right Profile users is to be patient. "There's lots of factors to consider, so don't let them overwhelm you. That's one reason why it's vital to include your colleagues in creating these profiles. As you use them, make sure you're able to confirm that candidates have all of the Dealmakers and none of the Dealbreakers. Follow the plan and don't let your personal feelings overrule the obvious. And be sure to follow the 'rules,' especially the one about never changing the details in the midst of the interview process."

Using Completed Hire-Right Profiles

Once completed, Hire-Right Profiles shape the remaining steps of the Talent Accelerator Process. The following four rules will help you get the most from your completed profiles:

Rule #1: Never Change Hire-Right Profiles in the Midst of Interviews

When a candidate seems to be a great fit but is missing one Dealmaker, it's normal to want to adjust the profile to match the person. The same is true with Dealbreakers—but each one was listed for a reason. Sticking with what's on a Hire-Right Profile ensures that you hire logically instead of emotionally.

Rule #2: Use Hire-Right Profiles as a Checklist, Providing One to Every Person Interviewing a Candidate

Hire-Right Profiles ensure that your team misses nothing. How? Each interviewer checks off criteria they witness during their interactions, confirming that prospective new hires match every Dealmaker and have none of the Dealbreakers.

Rule #3: Update Hire-Right Profiles to Increase Their Accuracy

Each round of hires can provide details that improve the accuracy of future Hire-Right Profiles. Review the performance of new hires two to three months after the start of their employment. Use their successes and struggles to add details to the profile.

Rule #4: Be Specific

Specific criteria are easier to understand and identify than generalities. For instance, listing a "drama-filled life" as a Dealbreaker might confuse interviewers. It's too ambiguous. Instead, describe specific behaviors, such as "complains daily about the latest difficulty or injustice."

Facts Over Feelings

During my "interviews" with potential relationship partners, my Dating-Right Profile made it easier to know who did and didn't fit my needs. But that was just the start; it helped me through each step of the dating process. It served as my guide on who to date, informed the questions I asked of each person, and ensured I never compromised my values nor allowed my emotions alone to run the show.

Your Hire-Right profiles will do the same for you. You'll rely on these candidate blueprints in each step of the Talent Accelerator Process. They'll guide you in selecting resources for procuring better talent. You'll use them to write compelling content for employment ads and job postings. They'll help you craft provocative questions that elicit the details needed to make accurate hiring choices. Hire-Right Profiles help you get away from hiring by gut. Facts become more important than feelings, resulting in hires who do good work.

Action List for Chapter 3

Incorporating Hire-Right Profiles into your selection process takes minutes when you follow these steps.

Prioritize Your Jobs

People often choose one of two paths to begin: the easy road or the vital one. The easy road to creating your first Hire-Right Profile is by picking a familiar role, one where you and your colleagues have lots of hiring experience. You may elect the vital path by choosing a job that is especially important to your company or department. Neither path is wrong. The most important thing is to make a choice and create your first profile, knowing that making progress is more important than choosing perfectly.

Create Your First Hire-Right Profile

Use the four questions for adding your hiring criteria to complete each quadrant. Start with the top half of the profile. If you find it easier to start with Dealmakers, begin there. What if you'd rather start with Dealbreakers? Go for it. After completing the top half, move on to the bottom portion for Boosts and Blocks. Write down everything that comes to mind, knowing that you can move items, delete criteria, or add information at any time. Keep focusing on progress, not perfection.

Review and Include Recommended Criteria

Consider the recommended assets listed earlier in this chapter and in Appendix B. Include only those that fit your organization's needs.

Involve Key Colleagues

Select at least three colleagues to independently create their own Hire-Right Profiles for the same role. Ideally, this occurs at the same time you're creating your own version. When three other colleagues aren't available, look outside your company. This could include vendors or service providers who've interfaced with people in the role for which you are creating a Hire-Right Profile.

Research When Needed

Use resources, such as the job description websites listed in this chapter, when creating Hire-Right Profiles for new jobs. You may also find these resources helpful if you are stuck when trying to complete a profile for an existing role.

Compare and Combine

Review your Hire-Right Profile alongside those of your colleagues. When a trait appears three or more times, that detail should always be included in the correct section of a completed profile.

Follow the Do's and Don't's

Don't change Hire-Right Profiles in the midst of interviews or use vague labels. Do create Hire-Right Profiles that are used as checklists by each interviewer, updating them 60 to 90 days after each round of hiring. Keep your candidate blueprints current, refreshing the content as the needs of your company evolve.

Step #2—
Improve Candidate Gravity

Generate a Continuous Flow
of Quality Candidates

Not all recruiting methods are equal. Some give you outstanding candidates for a modest effort. Others are labor intensive, producing hundreds of people, many of whom are a poor fit. Using the correct recruiting methods is essential if you want to efficiently hire better employees.

Picking the best talent-finding options can be a challenge. There are lots of ways to recruit, including job boards, social media, advertising, and requesting referrals. New innovations, improved technologies, and an expanding range of service offerings are added every year.

Some talent resources require a sizeable investment. Marta, a talent acquisition executive for a large financial institution, found this to be the case with job boards. She couldn't believe her eyes when her company's primary job board sent her a renewal quote. The same level of service was going to cost nearly double. She tried to negotiate a better deal, gaining a few concessions and a slightly lower price. Unfortunately, this lower price was still not within her budget. "I'm not sure what to do," she said. "We've been using that job board for a decade. It's one of our top resources. But, every year, it's gotten increasingly expensive."

I asked her what makes it a top resource. "Our recruiters have relied on it more than any other recruiting tool," she replied. "That why it's such a hard decision. I can't make the numbers work, but I also can't afford to let it go."

"Since you can't afford to let the board go," I said, "I assume it provides lots of good candidates." Making a face as though she'd bitten a lemon, Marta closed her door, leaned closer, and in a near whisper said, "What I'm about to say isn't politically correct, but that board brings in a ton of candidates, many of whom are garbage. We waste so much time reviewing resumes of people who don't fit."

Marta's experience isn't unique. You, too, have likely gotten poor results from certain recruitment methods. Does that mean that these methods are a waste of time? No. The issue is how they're being used. To hire efficiently, you need a healthy talent flow. Generating a continuous flow of quality candidates requires using the right resources in the right way.

Post and Pray

Many sources provide a generous flow of quality talent. However, no one source can be the do all, end all. Each resource ebbs and flows. That's why these resources must be used in the proper combination.

As we looked closer, Marta's situation had two issues. First, her team relied too heavily on this single job board. Second, they handled it incorrectly. "Marta," I said, "your recruiters are using a common yet unfortunate practice called 'post and pray.' They post open positions, then pray for responses."

Marta chuckled, "That's spot on. They've been posting and praying for years. I'm guessing that's because it does produce candidates. However, never enough and never quickly enough. I've talked to the team about pipelining talent before we need it. But they've been resistant."

The status quo is sticky. Like a spider's web, it's a trap. You get stuck in current circumstances. The longer you've done something, the more likely you are to repeat it.

I suggested to Marta that the time for talking was done. Instead, it was time to act. "I'm part of the problem," she said. "You've told me you can't think your way into change. You can only act your way into change. If my team is going to see things differently, it will be through action. How do you recommend we do that?" This began a discussion about the alternative to post and pray.

Plan and Produce

Waiting until a job opens to search for talent keeps you stuck in the old way of hiring. Many organizations hire in this manner, duking it out with one another over a limited candidate supply. Often, they're fighting over leftover third-tier talent.

"Passivity is our problem," said Marta. "When we wait to recruit, our results are inconsistent. We sometimes find decent people. Other times, we don't. We end up battling other organizations for the best of the three 'un's'—the best of the unhappy, unemployed, and underqualified. It costs us too much time and effort."

Shifting from reactive to active recruiting is an important step to hiring faster. However, recruiting actively isn't enough when you're searching for quality talent in a sea of "un's." You need a clear distinction between qualified and unqualified candidates.

Marta incorporated the Hire-Right Profile, working with hiring managers to create a clear picture of who was the best fit. She used that information to write improved posts for the job board, adding details that had been previously overlooked. The Hire-Right Profile also guided her in selecting better ways to recruit. "Never again will I be left flat-footed," she said. "Relying heavily on our primary job board has never been a good idea. Our poor results prove it. We need a constant flow of candidates if we're going to eliminate hiring delays."

When Marta introduced these improvements to her team, they were openly skeptical. They'd heard talk about change before, then nothing would happen. This time was different; we'd planned for their skepticism. Marta started by indicating that she was part of the problem, admitting she'd been all talk and little action. This got their attention, especially since she was taking the blame versus casting it on them. Marta went through reports on sources of talent, showing why they'd been struggling to fill jobs. By the time she finished explaining how they would be cultivating top talent and waiting for the right job to show up, the recruiters were like a sports team ready to take the field."

This is plan and produce. You create a plan to produce a continuous flow of qualified candidates. That flow is generated by tapping into an expanded pool of talent (Figure 4.1). The strength of your company's pull on top talent is called "candidate gravity."

Candidate Gravity

Drawing in people is a critical function in business. Stores that don't attract enough customers fail. Restaurants that don't fill tables close. Gyms that don't sell enough memberships fold. Companies with a weak pull on prospective job candidates always struggle to fill their open jobs.

Candidate gravity is the pull your organization has on talent. This pull may be weak, drawing in an insufficient supply of candidates; inconsistent, coming in ebbs and flows; or strong, generating a consistent stream of people. Companies with strong candidate gravity always draw a stronger flow of top talent their way, leaving second- and third-tier candidates for everyone else.

Eight streams of talent generate candidate gravity (Figure 4.1). Each one taps into a different pool of people.

Talent Stream #1: Advertising

Job ads are one of the oldest forms of recruiting. Yet, running such an ad isn't necessarily an old-school approach. Campaigns place targeted advertisements in the results of an Internet search engine. Banner ads on web pages are often viewed by hundreds of potential applicants. Numerous online magazines, newsletters, and classified ad sites offer you the ability to advertise job listings.

Old-school promotion still works. Each week, millions of people peruse job ads in printed publications. Flyers on bulletin boards at schools and houses of worship continue to attract applicants. Signs on buses and benches create awareness of job opportunities.

Advertising works when it delivers a persuasive message to the appropriate audience. Your ad content must be compelling

FIGURE 4.1   **Candidate Gravity**

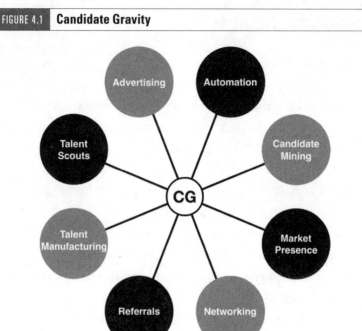

and succinct, communicating to readers what's in it for them to pursue a job at your company.

Talent Stream #2: Automation

Technology can generate talent and streamline your recruiting. Job boards and career sites come in many sizes and specialties. Sourcing systems find candidates for you. Automated telephone calling services alert job seekers to opportunities. Other recruiting tools find passive candidates or mass distribute job postings. We'll explore how to choose automation in Chapter 9.

Talent Stream #3: Candidate Mining

The longer a company has been around, the more resumes fill filing cabinets and databases. Many are covered in real or digital dust, having been overlooked for years. The resumes in these files are a rich, renewable source of potential hires and people who can provide referrals.

Mining this untapped pool of talent is a simple exercise. Methodical searches of databases convert old resumes into new leads. Working through a filing cabinet a few files a day reestablishes contact with potential hires and referral sources. Searching previous candidates in applicant tracking systems could uncover prospective employees and networking contacts.

Talent Stream #4: Market Presence

Your company has a presence. This presence is created by your physical locations, online identity, organization's reputation as a place to work, and overall standing in the community.

Market presence can draw in top talent. Storefront signs can convey organizational values. Websites can share stories of how employment at your company has lifted careers. Videos on social media can highlight where your organization stands on important issues.

Talent Stream #5: Networking

In the old days, if you wanted to network, you had to leave your house. You'd drive or fly to a conference, job fair, or reception. Today, you can also network virtually. Social media, online communities, and comments on articles have all become places for us to connect.

Getting the most from networking requires participation in both the physical and virtual worlds. Joining conversations on a discussion board before a conference leads to meaningful interactions at the event. Staying in touch with people on social media after a job fair may deepen relationships. Attending cocktail parties at the local chamber still offers opportunities to meet people who aren't active online. Colleges and schools are prime territory for connecting with talented people who have fresh perspectives. Full-scale networking taps into a wide stream of people who can become your job candidates and provide referrals to top talent.

Talent Stream #6: Referrals

Referrals have always been the most potent talent stream. One person can guide us to many others, pointing out who's particularly good at a job.

We have many opportunities to ask for referrals to potential job candidates. Current employees, along with their family and friends, can connect us to thousands. Every candidate interviewed by your company can be a source of introductions to colleagues and friends. Reference checks also provide us ready-made opportunities to ask for help with referrals.

Talent Stream #7: Talent Manufacturing

Job candidates aren't just found; they're also made. How? Through "talent manufacturing" programs like internships and education, which provide potential hires with experience and new skills; and cross-training programs, which provide current employees with the skills needed for advancement.

Of all the streams, talent manufacturing is the most underutilized.

Talent Stream #8: Talent Scouts

Actors on stage and screen have agents, professionals who land them their next roles. So, too, do people in every profession. Staffing firms and recruitment agencies are external corporate talent scouts, providing contract workers and full-time hires. The staffing industry has evolved into an entire ecosystem of services to help your company procure one person or an entire team of people.

Picking a solution from this ecosystem can be daunting. Chapter 10 is dedicated to this topic.

Only 10 percent of organizations across the globe maintain strong candidate gravity. Why? They maximize all eight of the talent streams; the other 90 percent do not. If you want your company to have stronger candidate gravity, you must identify where your pull on talent is weak and improve those areas of weakness.

Improving Candidate Gravity

Answers to common questions will show you how the process of improving candidate gravity works:

1. Why is our candidate gravity weak or inconsistent?

    It's important to remember that each talent stream gives you access to a different group of candidates. Some of the talent streams provide overlapping access to the same candidates, but no single stream can secure every qualified individual. If your company is experiencing an inconsistent flow of qualified candidates, you're not using all eight streams effectively.

    Marta's talent acquisition team wasn't in the habit of asking everyone for referrals, nor were they regularly participating in networking opportunities. Improving these two streams brought in top talent they hadn't previously found using their primary job board.

2. How does our organization improve a talent stream?

   Improving the flow of talent in each stream requires choosing the correct methods. For example, there are many automation options, including products from Indeed, LinkedIn, Monster, and CareerBuilder. Referrals can be generated using different techniques, such as querying current employees or asking for referrals during candidate reference checks. Picking the correct methods, in the form of resources and techniques, maximizes the flow from each of the eight streams of talent.

   The recruiters on Marta's team began asking for referrals in every reference check. They also launched different referral initiatives, including asking for leads from current and past job candidates, internal staff, and the friends and family of team members.

3. What makes a resource or technique the right one for us?

   Finding qualified people for a specific role requires tapping into the groups of people who may fit the role. Hire-Right Profiles will guide you in choosing methods for producing prospective employees from these talent pools.

   The Hire-Right Profile Marta created for one of the company's core roles, financial analysts, included two important Dealmakers: Active industry connections and strong verbal and listening skills. Recruiters researched options for finding people with these Dealmakers, looking for possibilities among the talent streams they weren't using effectively, including networking. They found several monthly networking opportunities widely attended by financial analysts that fit the bill.

4. How do you know you're using a resource or technique properly?

That's simple. If a resource is giving you a flow of qualified candidates, some of whom become good hires, you're using that resource correctly. An inconsistent flow from a resource indicates that you're likely making a mistake.

Two recruiters in Marta's firm generated a flood of financial analyst candidates from referrals. The rest of the team, in comparison, was drawing a trickle of talent. The success of the two recruiters stemmed from how they were asking for referrals. They made specific requests, based upon whom they were speaking with. Currently employed financial analysts were asked for referrals to colleagues at other firms. Requests of internal staff were focused on who they'd like to see join the company. Once the rest of the team adopted these practices, everyone had success in bringing in a steady flow of candidates from referrals.

5. Do we really need to use all eight streams to achieve strong candidate gravity?

Most organizations find they need to use all eight to maintain a strong talent flow, especially since each stream draws in candidates unique to that stream. Small companies, though, are the exception. As long as they leverage the most potent stream—referrals—smaller organizations can often generate a robust flow from four or five streams. The leveraging of this selection of talent streams is handled by managers, an HR leader, the business owner, or a combination of these individuals.

Marta and her team initially found the idea of using all eight streams overwhelming. In a short time, they discovered that employing all eight streams takes less effort than relying on only a few. Why? They were drawing candidates from a wider audience rather than struggling over a limited pool.

Maximizing each talent stream creates a continuous flow of talent. How do you create and sustain this flow? By using recruiting methods correctly, consistently, creatively, and completely.

The Human Aspect of Referrals

Why are referrals such a potent source of talent? Human nature. We were built to help each other.

Research demonstrates that helping one another is nature, not nurture. Social experiments at the Max Planck Institute for Evolutionary Anthropology found that children as young as 18 months old will help complete strangers. The researchers developed scenarios where an adult needed help, such as grasping for a clothes peg that had fallen to the floor. Virtually all the children handed the peg to the adult. These diaper-wearing toddlers lacked the socialization that teaches many life skills, yet they were already exhibiting altruistic behaviors.[1]

Altruism, our default factory programming, is why requesting referrals works. Each person we ask gets to help three people—their colleagues, us, and themselves. They get to do what they were born to do.

Are you in the habit of asking everyone for referrals? Probably not. Many people haven't developed the habit of

(continued)

asking for this type of help from every person they meet. Rather than viewing this as a natural human activity, you may believe it's an imposition or that the person being asked won't know anyone.

In politics, we often hear about the power of the people. In business, there's also a power within individuals—the power of their network. We are more connected than ever through the Internet and social media. Hundreds if not thousands of contacts are within our reach. That's why asking everyone is important: We never know whom someone may know.

How can you ask for referrals without sounding awkward or needy? Here's a simple four-step approach:

Step 1: Ask for help.

Requesting help taps into your shared humanity.

Step 2: Explain why.

Briefly explain why you are asking. Understanding your motives makes it easier for people to be supportive.

Step 3: Define who.

Be specific. People have lots of contacts. Asking for referrals for a specific type of person helps them search their vast mental Rolodex.

Step 4: Make your request.

Ask a short open-ended question to solicit their recommendations.

Put together, the four steps could sound like the following:

"May I get your help? I'm responsible for finding people who may fit our company—now or in the future. That's why I'd like your help. I'm looking to connect with people who have a background in [INSERT AREA OF EXPERTISE]. Who do you suggest I speak with?"

The Four Cs

Why does a recruiting method fail to supply enough talent? Often, the method gets the blame. However, it's usually the people who have failed to use it properly. To generate a flow of talent that's continuous, each recruiting method must be used correctly, consistently, creatively, and completely (Figure 4.2).

Correctly: Is the Method Being Used Correctly?

There's a right way and a wrong way. The right way (often referred to as a best practice) is the one that gives you the best results for the least effort.

Take job boards, for example. Marta's team previously spent hours sifting through job-board resumes of people who didn't fit. This unstructured and exhausting approach produced only a handful of acceptable candidates, never enough to fill all of their open positions.

Marta and her team eliminated the need for all that mindless sifting by planning ahead. They posted positions on job boards before the real need came up. Dealmakers from Hire-Right Profiles were added to better communicate who should apply. The number of matching candidates grew as the volume of applicants decreased.

Consistently: Do People Use It Consistently?

Properly using a recruiting method that fits your circumstances always increases the flow of talent, as long you apply that method consistently. Lack of consistency is the most common issue among the four Cs.

The referral initiative developed for Marta's team focused on consistency. Called "Engage Everyone," the initiative operated on the belief that every individual knows at least one person who

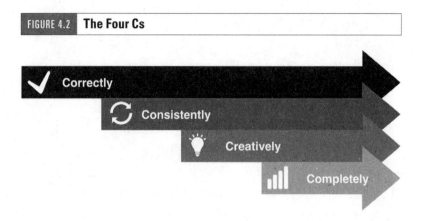

FIGURE 4.2   **The Four Cs**

could be a potential employee or source of candidate leads. This effort paid off: 85 percent of people provided at least one referral. Four new hires generated from Engage Everyone started with the company within two months.

Creatively: Are They Using It in Creative Ways?

Best practices are proven methods that are meant to be repeated. Creating twists on these proven ideas makes it easier to sustain these methods.

Marta noticed that networking and referrals were generating the strongest flows of candidates and the most new hires. To leverage this success, we designed the "Collaborative Community" campaign. The goal was to partner with leaders in centers of worship, community organizations, and other groups that provide help to their members. Leaders in many of these organizations were happy to participate. Job notices were placed on bulletin boards, announcements were made from pulpits, and recruiters were invited to attend a variety of events. Leads from Collaborative Community led to a dozen hires during the campaign's first six months.

Completely: Is the Method Being Used Completely, to Its Full Capacity?

An improved flow of candidates in a talent stream can have unintended consequences. It's normal that you'll become satisfied with better results and overlook untapped potential.

Marta collaborated with her firm's marketing and PR department as part of her sourcing strategy. Together, they fortified the company's market presence. Videos of new hires sharing about their job successes were posted on YouTube and social media. A podcast series was launched featuring employees sharing heartwarming stories about their tenure at the company. The website was upgraded, making it easier for qualified candidates to have immediate contact with a recruiter. Each of these methods proved beneficial, keeping the company top of mind and generating quality candidates.

During a progress review meeting, Marta proudly reviewed the successes resulting from their enhanced market presence. I congratulated her on this progress and asked when she planned on leveraging her company's physical locations as a recruitment method. After a moment of silence, Marta laughed, admitting she'd forgotten all about that idea. "It's so easy to be satisfied with current results," she said. "In some ways, satisfaction is a trap."

A contest soliciting inspirational quotes from employees provided content for banners and signs, which were displayed inside and out of the company's physical locations. These drew in additional candidates, one of which became one of the best hires of the year. "Had we continued to overlook using our market presence to its full capabilities," said Marta, "we wouldn't have found that candidate."

The four Cs are an indispensable tool. They'll guide you in determining why a recruiting method is failing and how to fix it.

They'll also help you implement new methods correctly the first time around.

Increasing Your Organization's Candidate Gravity

Given all the ways to recruit, the thought of using more of them may feel overwhelming to you. That's normal. You're probably already managing a full desk and a packed calendar. The thought of doing one more thing may seem impossible.

Improving candidate gravity takes time, but less than you might expect. Expanding one talent stream at a time immediately draws in new candidates. When you're ready to move to the next stream, you do so, expanding the capacity of each at your pace. After you implement recruiting methods, managing them becomes part of the daily routine.

This is why candidate gravity works in organizations of all sizes. It meets you where you are today and grows at a pace that works for you. Over time, the stronger flow from each talent stream increases candidate gravity, providing more candidates with less effort.

A timeline will help you stay on track and eliminate being overwhelmed. This tool defines deadlines, allowing you or your entire team to allocate time appropriately. The sample in Figure 4.3 was similar to the approach used with Marta's team. Every month was focused on improving a different talent stream and the methods that fed that stream. Prior to the beginning of each month, the four Cs were applied, allowing Marta to guide team members on what to improve and how to improve it. Specific actions were planned for each week of the month, such as adding referral generation to phone interviews one week and then to reference checks the following week.

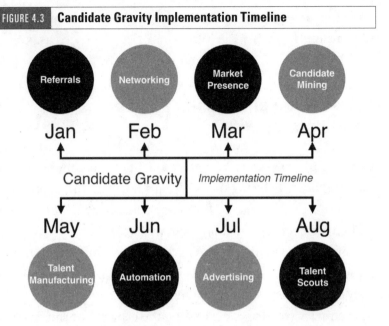

FIGURE 4.3   Candidate Gravity Implementation Timeline

Eliminating empty seats and long time-to-fill is all about people. The people in your company have to know who fits a job, and who does not. Then, talented people are lined up before they are needed. Strong candidate gravity supplies those people, empowering your company to cultivate qualified candidates and then wait for the right jobs to show up.

Action List for Chapter 4

To improve candidate gravity, take the following steps.

Review Your Core, Essential, and Supportive Roles

In the Action List for Chapter 2, I suggested prioritizing your jobs into three categories: core, essential, and supportive. Now is a good time to review and update your priority list before planning your approach to improving candidate gravity. The importance of some roles compared to others may have changed as market conditions and the needs of your company have changed.

Update Your Hire-Right Profiles

You'll use your Hire-Right Profiles to pick appropriate recruitment methods for improving talent streams. Ensure that Hire-Right Profiles are up-to-date and accurate before choosing any methods.

Take Stock

Understanding the current strength of your company's candidate gravity is important. A brief assessment will inform your efforts as you plan your improvement timeline.

Determine how many of the eight streams of talent are producing a strong flow of people. For any that are not, look at which recruitment methods are being used to add candidates to that stream. Are those methods being used correctly, consistently, creatively, and completely? Your goal in taking stock is to understand where your candidate gravity needs attention.

Pick Your Recruiting Methods

Different methods will provide access to different groups of people. Use your updated Hire-Right Profiles to pick these methods.

Ask your vendors of hiring technologies (like job boards and automated sourcing tools) for details on the effectiveness of their resource for your specific needs. Solicit proof, not promises. Whenever possible, request a free or low-cost evaluation period to experience how much effort is required in using the resource.

Spend some time noticing how your competitors are using their market presence to draw in candidates. Surf their company web pages, video and podcasting sites, and social media. Note ideas that you can borrow. Drive through town, paying close attention to how organizations use their physical location to attract job applicants.

Collaborate with your colleagues inside and outside your company for additional recruiting methods. Share and practice the four-step referral conversation, noted earlier in the chapter, with your colleagues. Ask for their suggestions for local networking opportunities, advertising media, and quality talent scouts.

Also, ask the people you recruit where they hang out. To which groups do they belong? Where do they get their news and share ideas online? Ask for invitations to join them at networking events.

Create a Timeline

Choosing the order in which you'll improve each stream will allow you to coordinate schedules and resources. A timeline template, similar to the one in Figure 4.3, is available for your use. You can download this template at the following website: resources.highvelocityhiring.com.

Where should you begin? Pick the stream that will immediately improve the flow of talent for your top core role. Address the other streams at a measured pace, allowing enough time to incorporate each into a regular recruiting routine.

Apply the Four Cs

The four Cs should guide how you improve each talent stream. Make certain everyone involved in using a recruiting method understands how to use it correctly. Define what constitutes consistency in employing that method. Schedule regular brainstorming sessions to develop and share creative ideas. Ensure that people are using the method completely, getting the most from their efforts.

Spot-check the flow of each of your talent streams a few times a month. Apply the four Cs if a flow drops, so you can swiftly address the problem.

Enroll Everyone in the Recruiting Effort

Improving candidate gravity is a team effort, especially when it comes to increasing the flow of talent in your referral and networking talent streams. Everyone in your company is connected to hundreds of people. Ask for their help to actively network and request referrals.

This requesting of referrals starts with the senior leaders. When senior leaders actively seek referrals, their leadership positively infects the rest of the company.

Create New Twists on Old Ideas

When recruiting, the third C, creativity, allows you to innovate. Experimenting with new twists on different methods keeps recruiting interesting and talent flowing.

One of the easiest ways to develop new approaches is by combining techniques. Here are three examples that combine networking and referrals:

- **Candidate recycling:** Invariably, good people will apply for jobs that don't suit them. Rather than casting these people aside, why not offer to introduce them to your colleagues at other companies?

- **Zombie searches:** Your resume files and candidate databases are likely filled with hundreds, if not thousands, of "lost" candidates whose contact details have become invalid. Rather than declaring these as dead ends, these talented prospects can be brought back to life using online search engines (such as zabasearch.com or pipl.com).

- **Orbiting businesses:** Whether it's a dry cleaner, sandwich shop, or florist, retailers strategically position themselves near centers of business. Ongoing networking with these establishments can attract their foot traffic as your future employees.

Keep Asking the Most Important Question

As your candidate gravity increases, keep asking: Are we generating a continuous flow of qualified candidates, some of whom become good hires, from each stream? If not, use the four Cs to resolve the issue.

Step #3—
Maximize Hiring Styles

Leverage Perception to Counter
Hiring Blindness and Support
Accurate Employee Selection

In the late 1990s, cognitive scientists Christopher Chabris and Daniel Simons created a video that later became an Internet sensation. As the video begins, an off-screen narrator asks the viewer to count how many times players wearing white T-shirts pass a basketball to one another. Making this simple job of counting more challenging, the three white T-shirted players dribble and pass the ball while maneuvering around three black-shirted players who are also dribbling and passing. After 30 seconds, the narrator asks, "How many passes did you count?" I tallied 15 passes—the correct answer. What I quickly learned, however, was that counting the passes wasn't the real point of the exercise. Instead, I discovered I had missed something when the narrator asked, "But did you see the gorilla?"

I thought this had to be a joke. But as I watched again, sure enough, there was a gorilla. Ten seconds into the action, a gorilla-costumed figure walked between the players, faced the camera, thumped its chest, and continued walking out of sight.[1] In their book, *The Invisible Gorilla*, the scientists report that half the viewers of the video missed seeing the faux primate. In some cases, viewers couldn't see the gorilla while looking directly at it. Such a perceptual phenomena is called "inattentional blindness," and occurs when we unintentionally ignore an object that was unexpected.[2]

Overlooking a gorilla in a video may not be overly concerning. However, if you're landing a plane and can't see that you're about to crash, that's a problem. That's exactly what happened at NASA's Ames Research Center. During extensive simulator training, seasoned commercial airline pilots "flew" simulated landings in varying weather conditions. After multiple sessions, a plane on the ground, called a "runway incursion," was added to the simulation. As pilots broke through a layer of clouds and prepared to land, some never saw the large plane in front of them entering the runway. One pilot, after being shown a video of his "fatal" attempt at landing, said, "If I didn't see [the tape], I wouldn't believe it. I honestly didn't see anything on that runway."[3]

These perceptual blind spots aren't limited to eyesight. People experience inattentional deafness as well. As an example, Chabris and Simons recount a social experiment by *Washington Post* columnist Gene Weingarten and virtuoso violinist Joshua Bell. With Stradivarius in hand, Bell performed for 43 minutes outside a Washington, D.C., subway station at rush hour. Out of more than a thousand passersby, Bell's virtuosity was only noticed by seven people. In 2008, Weingarten went on to win the Pulitzer Prize for Feature Writing for his cover story about the event. Bell netted just $52.17—the amount of cash thrown by those seven passersby into his open violin case. Why didn't more people notice the gifted Bell? The scientists' hypothesis: "[W]hen people are focusing attention (visual or auditory) on one task—getting to work—they are unlikely to notice something unexpected—a brilliant violinist along the way."[4]

If seasoned pilots can't see a giant airplane, and a thousand people can't hear heavenly music, and millions of viewers don't notice when a basketball drill is interrupted by a gorilla, just how much have we been missing when conducting something as ordinary and humdrum as a job interview?

The Invisible Gorillas of Interviewing

Many people have been disappointed when the candidates they interviewed ended up being poor hires. How did that happen? The interviewers say things like the following:

- "He interviewed so well. I thought he'd be able to do the job."

- "She seemed like a great fit, but in the end she never really fit in."

- "I'm still not sure how such an accomplished person could perform so badly."

- "He seemed like such a nice guy, but after we hired him he was a jerk. How'd I miss that?"

That last quote came from Simon, the vice president of a technology company in the eastern United States. His comment was about a recent hire, and this was not a unique experience. In fact, his "batting average," as he put it, was not good, and was the source of negative feedback on his last two performance reviews. "I'm one for three," said Simon dejectedly. "For every one person I get right, there are two who end up quitting or are fired within the first few months. I've got to figure out what I'm doing wrong or I'll be the one looking for a job."

I showed Simon the video from Chabris and Simons. He too didn't see the gorilla the first time around. Like many people, he was shocked he could miss something so obvious. As we discussed how the video related to hiring, I asked Simon, "Looking back at those failed hires, what were their 'gorillas'? In other words, during the interviews, what were the important unexpected details you missed?"

To say that Simon experienced an epiphany is an understatement. For the next ten minutes, he went down his mental list of failed hires, name by name, identifying misses that resulted from his "hiring blindness," a form of inattentional blindness. "Once people were onboard, the issues that showed up were just as blatant as those in the gorilla video," said Simon. "In the interviews, though, I was so focused on what I was expecting that I missed clear indications of future problems." As an example, Simon told me about a recent failed hire: "The candidate interviewed with a real 'edge' to him, and I thought that was a good thing. When I've hired other people with that kind of personality, it turned out well. I expected that would happen in this case, too. I, however, overlooked his sarcasm, which during the interview he used several times. It was right in front of me and I didn't notice."

Missing what later becomes obvious is common. Looking and listening does not mean that we take in all the pertinent information. Simon wondered how he could do better next time. That prompted an important discussion about dating.

Dating and the Invisible Gorilla

Anyone who's ever dated has experienced invisible gorillas. The gorillas in dating are bad personality traits and behaviors, appearing weeks or months into a relationship. Why does it take so long for these gorillas to show up? During the early weeks, people are on their best behavior. As they get comfortable, they lower their guard and let out different aspects of who they are.

Dating and interviewing, as I mentioned in Chapter 3, have lots in common. During interviews, job candidates are on their best behavior as they tell, sell, and swell:

- They tell interviewers what they believe the interviewers want to hear.

- They sell the best parts of their work history and abilities.

- They swell the egos of decision makers through praise.

Does this mean that everyone being interviewed engages in deceit? Absolutely not. It is natural that people disclose only those aspects that will land them the job. The problem is that this very human behavior interferes with good fit. That's a key reason why so many hires fail: In essence, the person hired is not the same one interviewed.

The primary difference between dating and interviewing is that interviewers usually don't have years to get to know someone before "proposing." Which is why Simon, like everyone who conducts interviews, needs to understand his own personal hiring style.

Hiring Styles

Your personality, expertise, and experiences shape your approach to leadership and how you select talent. How you select talent is called your "hiring style." Hiring styles come in four types (Figure 5.1):

- **The Tackler:** Tacklers are defined by speed and decisiveness. They want to be in control and reach goals quickly. When conducting an interview, they get to the point and appreciate people who do the same. Tacklers tend to hire those candidates who, they believe, can condense timelines and hit targets fast.

- **The Teller:** Tellers are characterized by their talkativeness. They focus on using their communication skills to motivate. In interviews, they spend appreciable time speaking, often selling the candidate on the company and its opportunities. Tellers frequently hire candidates who they believe will be inspired to act upon what the Teller has said.

- **The Tailor:** Tailors prize collaboration. They're the ones who point out that there's no "I" in "team." During interviews, they take time for rapport-building, conversation, and the open exchange of thoughts and feelings. Tailors are likely to hire candidates capable of cultivating strong working relationships.

- **The Tester:** Testers are methodical. They make decisions through data and other tangible forms of proof. While interviewing candidates, they gather pertinent details and value facts over stories. Testers tend to hire candidates who share logical evidence that demonstrates they are the right fit for the job.

FIGURE 5.1   **The Four Hiring Styles**

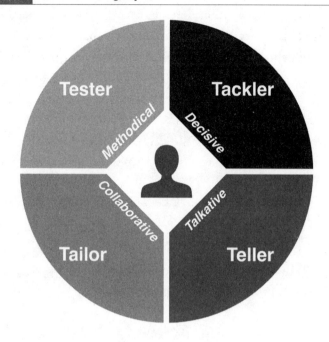

The good news is that none of these styles is bad. The bad news, however, is that if we're too reliant on our dominant style, it can keep us excessively focused on one part of reality. It can create distortion.

When I shared the four hiring style descriptions with Simon, he agreed how easy it is to look past what's right in front of you: "I'm a born Tackler. I like things done yesterday. It's no wonder I've been missing things." Knowing that I always ask for examples, he went on to say, "Take that edgy guy who ended up being a jerk. I was so focused on what I was trying to get done in my department that I zeroed in on his succinct answers. That's why I never noticed his blatant aggressive sarcasm. It was only after he began interacting with other employees that I realized my mistake."

Simon then had a greater epiphany: "Wait, that's how I'm going to get better at interviewing, isn't it? I not only need to be aware of the limitations of my hiring style, but I need to include other colleagues who are dominant in one of the other three styles."

What Is Your Personal Hiring Style?

People often have one of the following reactions when they first read about hiring styles:

- They believe they've discovered their dominant style.

- They suspect they have more than one dominant style.

- They're not sure any of the styles fit them perfectly.

Just as everyone has a dominant hand or leg, so too does everyone have a dominant approach to hiring, whether they realize it or not.

The following three discovery exercises can help you determine your primary, personal hiring style.

Exercise #1: Dating and Hiring

Given the similarities between dating and interviewing, think about how you behaved with each person you've dated. Which hiring style showed up most?

Exercise #2: The Last Five Hires

Share the four hiring style descriptions with the last five people you've hired. Ask each which style best describes you.

Exercise #3: Three Acquaintances

Select three acquaintances. Avoid family and close friends, as their concern for you could prejudice them. Provide them with the hiring styles descriptions. Ask each which hiring style best describes you.

If one or more of the exercises identifies a single style as dominant, you're now ready to maximize your personal hiring style. The next section of the chapter shows you how.

(continued)

If the results conflict or are inconclusive, that's not unusual. Many people have learned to use their nondominant hand. Yet, they're still apt to favor their dominant one. The same is true of hiring styles.

When two or more styles appear equally dominant, carefully watch for which style you favor during future interviews. That will be your dominant style.

Leveraging Hiring Styles

A team composed of people with diverse hiring styles gives you a more expansive and realistic perspective than if your team were composed of people with one or two styles. To assemble a diverse team, begin by identifying three people with hiring styles different than your own. Before conducting an interview, coordinate your team's efforts. To best leverage each hiring style, your team should have a discussion that answers the following questions:

- "What are my style's blind spots? What other styles can better see what I'm not seeing?"

- "What past hiring mistakes have we made repeatedly? How will the hiring team use its combined styles to avoid those mistakes?"

- "What do we need to know about a candidate? How can we uncover that information? Which styles are best suited for spotting those details?"

To leverage each style during an interview, team members should pay special attention to details that tap into their innate perceptions. For example:

- The Tackler watches for evidence of the candidate's drive.

- The Tailor notices how the candidate collaborates.

- The Tester looks for details that prove the candidate can do the job, if hired.

- The Teller shares a few things about the job and company, gauging the candidate's reaction to that information.

This team approach reduces effort and increases hiring speed. Instead of separate interviews that consume most of the day, a brief screening interview by phone is followed by one hands-on interview with the hiring team. (You'll read more about these interviews in Chapter 6.) With all four styles in the room, interviewers rarely miss anything that's important or unexpected.

Expertise Is the Key

After implementing a hiring team that leveraged all four hiring styles, Simon experienced much better results. Instead of two out of every three people quitting or being fired within a few months, new-hire success rose to 90 percent. Tenures of these improved hires were two years or longer. Simon's subsequent performance review praised his progress. He was even chosen to lead internal sessions to share a case study about his hiring team.

These results are neither surprising nor atypical. While working with thousands of leaders across the globe, I've watched them leverage hiring styles to take in more information and make fast and accurate hires. Why does this happen? The "invisible gorilla" researchers, Chabris and Simons, found that there is one way to accurately predict how likely someone is to see the unexpected—through expertise:

Expertise helps you notice unexpected events, but only when the event happens in the context of your expertise. Put experts in a situation where they have no special skill, and they are ordinary novices, taxing their attention just to keep up the primary task.[5]

By implementing an approach that leverages all four hiring styles, companies maximize the expertise that comes with each style. Interviewers see the unexpected and hear what's important, thereby improving accuracy and increasing hiring speed.

Action List for Chapter 5

To understand and improve your hiring style, take the following steps.

Determine Your Hiring Style

Review the four hiring style descriptions mentioned earlier in this chapter. What was your first reaction as to which one best fits how you behave in interviews? This is most likely your primary hiring style.

Validate Your Hiring Style

Use one or more of the discovery exercises in the What Is Your Personal Hiring Style? section to confirm your primary hiring style. Also, if you're uncertain which of the four styles is dominant for you, these exercises will help.

Teach the Hiring Styles

Educate direct reports and colleagues on hiring styles. This will help you integrate these ideas and deepen your own knowledge, while helping others understand and benefit from them. If you have no direct reports, or if you work alone, teach friends, neighbors, or family how to identify and maximize their personal hiring style.

Create a Hiring Team

Select three people whose dominant styles differ from each other's and your own. They'll be your hiring teammates. The four of you should then conduct interviews by using the framework in the Leveraging Hiring Styles section of this chapter. When three other teammates aren't available (for example, when you run a solo business), look outside of your company. Perhaps you could call upon one of your service providers, such as an attorney, banker, or accountant.

Also, some leaders create an advisory board in order to help with hiring. Board member selection takes into consideration acquiring people with contrasting hiring styles.

Step #4—
Conduct Experiential
Interviews

Employ Better Selection Methods
to Improve Precision and Speed

Conventional interviews don't work. Why? A job candidate is always on his best behavior. He tells you the right things and shares only the best parts of his background. Rather than painting a complete picture, a conventional interview narrows the lens, providing you with a mere glimpse of a person. This is why we're often disappointed when the person we interviewed is not the one who shows up on Monday morning.

The problem with conventional interviews doesn't stop there. During the interview, you're selling the prospective hire on your company and culture. But no matter how many rounds in the process, conventional interviews don't provide an accurate reflection of what it's like to work at your company each day.

For an interview to be effective, it can't be conceptual. Interviewing should be a reality check—a real and efficient experience that allows you and the candidate to make an informed decision. A decision based on facts. When armed with facts, each of us is capable of decisive action.

The Interview Experiment

My interviews weren't always focused and fast. Like many people, I was told I should be slow to hire and quick to fire. My mentors in the late 1980s modeled long interviews packed with questions. Candidates making it out of round one went through more of the same in round two, with a third round added for really important hires. All in effort to get hiring right the first time.

Problem was, this slow approach was doing more harm than good. Work was piling up and good candidates were being lost to competitors. When hires were made, some worked out; many did not. Those that failed on the job had excelled during interviews. Our process was a crapshoot. Multiple rounds of exhaustive interviews were ending up with mixed results and exhausted managers. Less than half of the people hired lasted more than a year.

One day, out of sheer frustration, I decided to try something different. I'd been interviewing a candidate for a sales role. His background was impressive with almost a decade selling telecommunications equipment. Our phone screening went well; meeting him in person was the next stage.

Instead of putting him through our litany of questions during a face-to-face interview, I had him spend our entire time together selling. I introduced him to three people from other companies in our building. He had one task: Sell. All three buyers were open to considering new telecom products. If he didn't land our sales job, his time was still well spent, giving him three opportunities to grow his current book of business.

In less than 90 minutes, I had my answer. He was not a fit for our job. The guy that showed up on the telephone was different from the salesperson I observed in action. He had great answers to questions in the phone screening, coming across as warm and affable. However, what he told me about his approach to selling and how he actually sold were different. In the three sales meetings, he was surly and pushy. Not the kind of person who would do well in our company.

Had I followed our process of multiple rounds of interviews, I would've had a conceptual experience. The candidate would have continued his tell, sell, and swell. I would've spent hours on someone who would've interviewed well but become a hiring disaster.

Instead, I'd invested less than two hours between the phone screening and a hands-on interview. I experienced the real person and saw and heard how he behaved when it counts—doing the work. The right decision, not to hire him, was clear and obvious. It was based upon factual evidence of how he performed as a salesperson versus the inaccurate picture he painted on the telephone.

The only question I had after the interview was how to apply this approach to different types of roles. It was relatively easy to let a salesperson sell and experience it being done. I had to develop ways to create real experiences that allowed me to see people in other jobs in action.

Experiential Interviews

I spent two years designing and testing "experiential," or hands-on, interviewing. These interviews had to accomplish two things. First, they needed to determine if a candidate could do quality work. Second, they needed to show whether or not the candidate could work well with others.

I was picky about whom I'd meet, only interviewing someone if they matched the Hire-Right Profile. During an initial phone interview, I reviewed their abilities, communication skills, and personality-fit for our culture. A brief conversation determined who was worth bringing in for a hands-on interview.

The hands-on interview was divided into two parts. The first part was focused on having the candidate do sample work. Computer programmers were given specs, so they could write computer code. Accounting candidates analyzed financials. Marketing staffers designed a promotional campaign. Recruiters were provided sample jobs to fill. For each type of role, I developed tasks to be done based on real workplace situations.

During the second part, each candidate was joined by members of our staff. This gave me the opportunity to watch how they interacted with potential coworkers. I gave them a problem to solve or a question to answer as a team. Programmers had to work together to debug code that was crashing a system. Accounting candidates had to work with several members from the accounting department to trace errors in financial reports. Marketers participated in a brainstorming session on a marketing campaign. Recruiters had to collaborate with a hiring manager to plan the hiring process.

While all of this was happening, I was an observer. Joining me were several other leaders, each with a different hiring style. We quietly made notes of what we experienced. Debriefs after each hands-on interview allowed us to compare notes about how people matched up to our Hire-Right Profile. Reference checks were then used to affirm that the candidate had all of the Dealmakers and none of the Dealbreakers.

The results were groundbreaking. Interviews were shorter and more effective. We could see proof of whether or not candidates were good fits for a role and experience how they'd fit in. Our hands-on interview showed us how a candidate worked and interacted.

The leaders who had doubts about this new way of interviewing quickly bought in. As one put it, "Seeing is believing. Interviews have always seemed like a form of gambling. Sometimes I got lucky. Others times I did not. Being able to see someone in action makes this new form of interviewing far more accurate."

Initially, I was concerned how candidates would be affected by having observers in the room. Would these people be a distraction? No. Candidates told us that after ten minutes they forgot the observers were there. The work kept their attention, allowing them to tune out the others.

Even the candidates themselves gave this new type of interview a thumbs-up. They got to experience the job and the team. Also, they liked how quickly they could determine whether the job was what they were looking for.

One of my biggest surprises was how experiential interviews engaged passive candidates (people not actively seeking a new job). Many passive candidates had previously balked at participating in a conventional interview. That was not the case when we allowed these candidates to "try out" a job. Passive candidates not only chose to participate, but often asked to join our company as soon as we could hire them.

After two years, the process was perfected. Hiring was a four-stage process: reviewing candidate documents, conducting brief phone interviews, one in-person hands-on interview, and reference checks. It no longer took weeks to hire one person. Now we could do it in a matter of hours. Most important, our new-hire success rate skyrocketed. Ninety-five percent of our new hires stayed for at least a year.

The Four Stages of Experiential Interviews

Today, thousands of companies across the globe engage in experiential interviewing. Regardless of industry, the process stages are completed in the same order (Figure 6.1).

Stage 1: Compare the Candidate's Written Materials to Your Hire-Right Profile

You'll compare each candidate to your Hire-Right Profile. To do this, you'll use resumes or job applications plus, if needed, a few written questions. A candidate who has enough of the required skills, experience, and education listed under Dealmakers moves to Stage 2.

Stage 2: Conduct a Brief Phone Interview

A 20-minute (or less) phone conversation, for most roles, allows you to hear how the candidate communicates as you review their background and discuss the job. Also, this provides an opportunity to discover how their values, helpful behaviors, and personality features may or may not fit your company culture. If they match additional Dealmakers and have none of the Dealbreakers, they move to Stage 3.

Stage 3: Hold an In-Person Hands-On Interview

Here, you'll have the candidate do sample work (both on their own and with others). The hiring team, comprised of the four

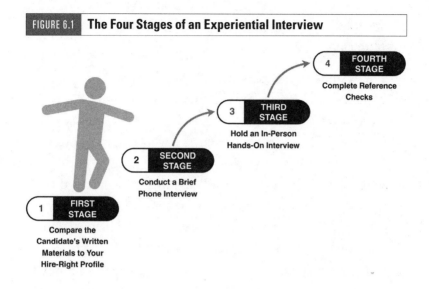

FIGURE 6.1   **The Four Stages of an Experiential Interview**

hiring styles, observes silently. They "check off" any Dealmakers, Dealbreakers, Boosts, and Blocks. If they determine that the candidate has none of the Dealbreakers and most, if not all, of the Dealmakers, the candidate moves to Stage 4.

Stage 4: Complete Reference Checks

Reference checks (and background checks, if required for the role) are used to affirm that the candidate has all of the Dealmakers, none of the Dealbreakers, and few, if any, Blocks. If they pass this last stage, they're offered a job immediately or the next time a seat opens.

A few additional notes:

- In Stage 3, I recommended that your candidate demonstrate their abilities by performing sample work. You also have the option to have them do real work; if you do so, however, you'll have to pay them and comply with labor laws. These working interviews pay the going rate for doing key aspects of the job.

For example, a southeastern U.S. hospital asks nursing candidates who reach Stage 3 to work with patients directly. According to the hospital administrator, this has allowed the hospital to attract better nurses, who end up as long-term employees. "When we first floated this idea, our legal and risk management teams thought we were crazy," the administrator said. "However, they got on board when we helped them understand that seeing a candidate in action actually lowered our risk. As a result, we now fill open jobs in less than an hour, and our patient outcome measures have improved significantly."

- Candidates who don't make it through the process are, whenever possible, referred to other employers. This goodwill gesture pays dividends, generating positive word-of-mouth advertising for your company.

The Flexibility of Experiential Interviews

Experiential interviews can be used for any type of role, yet the four stages remain the same. Each stage determines whether a candidate is a fit.

How do you apply experiential interviews to different industries and roles? Consider the following three examples.

Manufacturing

A midwestern U.S. manufacturer had ongoing problems in hiring machinists and welders. The company tried attracting candidates by improving its compensation plan. However, new hires didn't stay long when another organization offered them more money. To remedy this problem, the manufacturer implemented experiential interviewing.

In Stage 1, the manufacturer asked each candidate to email them a resume and submit an answer to the following question: "Under what circumstances would you consider changing jobs?" The answer, along with the resume, allowed company leaders to see if a candidate had both the correct skills and mindset. They were looking for candidates with transferable experience and motives that went beyond money, such as opportunities for career advancement or ongoing skill development.

Candidates who reached Stage 2 were interviewed by a company machinist or welder over the phone. These conversations, lasting 15 to 20 minutes, covered a lot of ground. The interviewers gained insights about a candidate's skills, behaviors, and personality. If a candidate had any of the Dealbreakers, Stage 2 is where they invariably showed up. When there were Dealbreakers, they'd end the process with that candidate.

Stage 3 was a joint hands-on interview: Two candidates were brought in simultaneously. They were given a single problem to solve together, such as fixing parts that been machined incorrectly. The interviewers watched how the pair interacted, noting how the candidates applied their skills, worked together, and solved the problem.

In Stage 4, the manufacturer checked references for candidates who passed Stage 3. As simple as this stage sounds, reference checks had always been a struggle. The reason: Previous employers would only confirm the most basic information, such as the individual's dates of employment. For more meaningful detail, the manufacturer contacted the candidate's former coworkers. These former colleagues were asked about the candidate, especially for experiences involving important Dealmakers and Dealbreakers.

Their answers enabled hiring managers to gather the last bits of evidence needed for a fully informed hiring decision.

The experiential interviewing methodology eliminated candidates motivated by money alone. It also made it easier to attract passive candidates. In under a year, the company went from too few candidates to a surplus ready to accept a job the moment one opened. This success prompted the manufacturer to expand its use of experiential interviews in hiring engineers and managers.

Executives

A global recruitment firm struggled for years in hiring executives. Four of the previous six executives lasted less than a year. These failed hires fit a pattern: Their leadership style was excessively authoritarian. Rather than collaborating, they made demands and gave orders. Two of the four were also caught lying.

Ending this pattern of poor hires became the recruitment firm's top priority. They began by creating Hire-Right Profiles that addressed the specific issues, adding Dealmakers, such as a collaborative leadership style, and Dealbreakers, such as lack of integrity.

During their next round of hiring, they experimented with experiential interviewing. In Stage 1, candidates were asked to provide a resume and answer written questions that delved into their leadership styles. Those who qualified for Stage 2 met by phone with several members of the hiring team. In addition to reviewing their background, the phone interview was used to discuss the pros and cons of collaboration.

The third stage was a hands-on strategy session with the candidate's prospective team of direct reports. The candidate was given full control of this meeting. If she wanted to ask questions of the team or assign prep work before the session, she did. She set the agenda and ran the meeting. It was her show. How she led and what they accomplished were reviewed by the hiring team, some of whom were part of the exercise.

Reference checks rounded out the fourth stage of the process, confirming she met all of the required criteria, especially integrity. Reference checks included people at different seniority levels at the candidate's previous employers. Each individual was asked for details of things they experienced, especially as they related to issues around integrity. Three potentially bad hires were averted as a result of details uncovered during this final stage.

Since implementation of experiential interviewing, the company has hired four executives, all of whom are still with the organization. The company's board has deemed these individuals the "best hires ever made" as a result of the work each has accomplished so far.

Customer Support

A Pacific Rim software company took months to hire a single customer service manager. One of the reasons why had to do with the customer service manager's daily work. Since helping customers took time, the software company felt a lengthy hiring process helpfully tested their candidates' patience. Was this assumption correct? Did a drawn-out hiring process lead to successful hires? No. Less than 10 percent remained with the company more than two years.

Many of these hires, who were tenured and successful support professionals, weren't coachable. They'd progress only as far as their current abilities took them. They'd get stuck, hitting a performance level below what was expected.

The software company replaced its drawn-out process with experiential interviewing. Hire-Right Profiles were created, adding "being coachable" as a Dealmaker. Telephone interviews zeroed in on examples of coachability. For instance, candidates were asked to share how they applied lessons learned from mistakes made in their current job.

The hands-on interview simulated some of the most challenging parts of the customer support job. Company employees played the role of "customer." The task of the candidate was to solve the "problem" being presented by this customer.

Halfway through the hands-on interview the senior vice president of customer relations would pause the process and provide feedback to the candidate. Then, the hands-on interview would resume. Observers met afterwards to review their experience and discuss how coachable the candidate was during the interview. If candidates matched all of the Dealmakers, they moved to the final stage. References were used to affirm that he fully matched the entire Hire-Right Profile.

Candidates who passed all four stages were offered a job immediately, if one was open, or as soon as one became available. Those hired became exceptional employees. They ramped up quickly and broke company records. Tenure for all but a few progressed well beyond the two-year mark. Best of all, all four stages of the process took under one week to complete.

Launching Questions

We all love to hear ourselves talk, and we appreciate when others listen to us. In interviews, we can use this to our advantage by asking better questions.

What makes a question better? When it's easily understood. Too often, our questions are confusing. We use too many words, overwhelming the listener.

There's a science to asking great questions. Questions posed in the right manner are easily understood, allowing listeners to think carefully about their answers. You

(continued)

can actually see this happen. When people are asked compelling questions, they pause, think, and then respond. Their response is thorough, accurate, and satisfying for everyone in the conversation.

The most effective manner of querying candidates is using "launching" questions. These provocative, open-ended questions are 12 words or less. Their brevity ensures that they are immediately understood, launching people into giving detailed answers. Launching questions create conversational quid pro quo: The questioner wants to understand, and the respondent gets to be heard. Every response can be turned into a new launching question, allowing you to develop an even deeper understanding of your candidate.

What do launching questions look like? Here are three such questions often used during a Stage 2 telephone interview:

- "Why us?"

    Motives are important. Knowing if your candidate is inspired by your company's mission or just needs a job will help you pick the best people.

- "Why now?"

    When a candidate is actively searching for a job, knowing what's driving that decision is important. Is the candidate desperate to make a change, ready to leap at the first offer? Or, is she happy and simply open to a new opportunity that could make life even better? Knowing what's driving someone's behavior is vital in choosing the right people for your company.

- "What job suits you best?"

    Too often, interviewers ask candidates about their perfect job. Such a question sets up the candidate and the employer for failure, since jobs and companies are rarely perfect. Instead of asking about perfection, ask about personal fit.

Launching questions are particularly important when you speak with passive candidates. Since these individuals

(continued)

aren't actively looking for work, engaging them in a meaningful conversation can be a challenge. Not so when using launching questions. For example, when someone says they aren't looking for a job, you could ask, "Under what circumstances would you consider something new?" If someone says they're happy in their current role, you could pose, "What would make you happier?" Both examples engage people in a conversation about possibilities.

Launching questions should be used in all of your interviews. You'll see examples of launching questions in this and other chapters.

Creating Your Experiential Interviews

How do you carry out an effective experiential interview? I'll walk you through the details.

Stage 1: Compare the Candidate's Written Materials to Your Hire-Right Profile

With your Hire-Right Profile in hand, you'll review a candidate's background. You'll look at their resume or job application. Also, you may choose to have them submit answers to written questions.

It's important to remember that resumes and job applications are summaries. It's rare that these summaries will allow you to determine whether someone matches your entire Hire-Right Profile. Instead, you'll select Dealmakers and Dealbreakers to help you determine who moves to Stage 2. How many Dealmakers and Dealbreakers are enough? You'll likely find that picking a few of each will suffice.

As an example, let's look at how one company assessed candidates for a sales role. To pass Stage 1, the hiring team chose two Dealmakers and two Dealbreakers from the Hire-Right Profile:

Dealmakers

Healthy overachiever, demonstrated by exceeding expectations consistently

Follows directions

Dealbreakers

Sells price instead of value

Misses deadlines regularly

The company had candidates submit resumes. These candidates were also given a deadline to answer these questions:

- "Why do you fit this job? Please keep your answer to a few sentences."

- "How do you sell? Be specific, but limit your response to two or three paragraphs."

- "In your most recent role, what expectations were you asked to meet? How consistently did you meet those? What specific steps did you take?"

Candidates who failed to meet the deadline and follow directions were dropped. Those whose resumes and written answers passed the Dealmakers-and-Dealbreakers test moved on to Stage 2.

Stage 2: Conduct a Brief Phone Interview

Your Stage 2 phone interview should focus on whether a candidate meets your company's needs and culture. You'll also notice how the candidate speaks and listens, and you'll get a sense of their personality. Your questions should lead them toward discussing topics important to your Hire-Right Profile.

One member of your hiring team should take the lead on the call. Other team members can listen in, helping to counteract hiring blindness. For staff level roles, a well-planned phone interview should take no more than 20 minutes. For executive jobs, plan on spending a maximum of 30 to 40 minutes.

Stage 3: Hold an In-Person Hands-On Interview

In Stage 3, you'll want to watch the candidate do the type of work they'd be doing if hired. This can be a realistic simulation or work-for-compensation. During part of the hands-on interview, have the candidate work with others, such as one or more of the following: Potential colleagues, members of your hiring team, other job candidates.

Pick aspects that prove the candidate can do quality work. How do you choose? Have them demonstrate important skills. Role-play difficult conversations. Present them with problems they'll need to solve.

An effective hands-on interview in Stage 3 can take as little as 60 minutes for staff positions. For senior and executive level roles, plan on up to two and a half hours.

Stage 4: Complete Reference Checks

Experiential interviewing is real, not conceptual. As a result, you'll often find you've verified every detail on a Hire-Right Profile by the end of Stage 3. If so, you may be ready to hire the candidate now or the moment you have an open seat. In other cases, there may be one or more Dealmakers or Dealbreakers that remain unconfirmed. Regardless of which situation you find yourself in, it's worth the investment to spend a few minutes on Stage 4. When you do, you'll increase your new-hire success rate by at least 20 percent.

There are three keys to success when conducting reference checks:

1. **Seek proof:** Whether you're questioning a reference giver about a candidate's Dealmaker or Dealbreaker, ask for proof. Don't stop at generalizations. Ask for a specific example.

2. **Request that reference givers provide additional contacts:** Smart candidates aren't likely to connect us with people who are going to say negative things. Ask each reference giver for the names of people who worked with the candidate. Contact these people, asking them for the proof you seek.

3. **Obtain at least one peer reference:** References are traditionally conducted with managers. Yet, managers usually spend limited time with their employees day-to-day. Managers may also be restricted by company policy as to what they can share. Peers, on the other hand, spend more time with prospective hires and may not be confined by the same rules.

Always Interviewing, Occasionally Hiring

Hiring faster made sense to Troy and Claudia. They co-led a department in a pharmaceutical company that always had open seats. Both agreed they needed better hiring profiles and stronger candidate gravity, and that hiring teams would help counter hiring blindness. We worked together, in collaboration with their talent acquisition team, to improve these three parts of their process.

Agreeing on how to interview—*that* was a different matter. Claudia hated conventional interviews and felt they were the cause for the department's failed hires. Troy, on the other hand, loved their process. Two phone interviews were followed by three separate face-to-face meetings. "We've crafted a great process. It includes behavioral interviewing and a 'Topgrading' assessment to spot top talent," he said. "I'm not willing to give up on a process that isn't broken. Our interviews work just fine."

There was no convincing Troy to give experiential interviewing a try, even after Claudia "whiteboarded" their poor hiring statistics. "Half our good candidates drop out of our long hiring process," said Claudia. "And, we're not meeting our MBOs (management by objectives) for employee turnover this year. By any measure, our interviewing process isn't just broken. It's beyond repair."

I'd been forewarned by their boss that Troy and Claudia were competitive. A hiring competition seemed like the right tool to help these two get unstuck from the status quo. Troy continued interviewing the old way; Claudia and I worked together to design and implement experiential interviewing. The rules of the contest were simple: Whoever filled the most jobs won. New hires had to pass their 90-day probationary period in order to count toward their hiring totals.

Who won? Claudia. It was a landslide. She hired four times as many people as Troy. He was stunned. "I figured she'd end up interviewing more people than I did," he said. "But I thought I'd win in the end by making more quality hires. Many of the people she added to the team have ended up being better employees than those I brought on board. With less effort, she made more hires."

The hiring contest had an added benefit: It filled all of the department's open seats. Claudia and Troy joined forces and began cultivating talent before it was needed by always interviewing and occasionally hiring. They generated an ongoing flow of candidates, inviting those that looked like a fit for interviews. In a short time, they built an inventory of people who were ready to join the company when a job opened.

"One of my biggest surprises," said Troy, "is how an active approach to hiring has made us a more attractive employer. We're like a Broadway show that's sold-out. The fact that it's hard to get in creates buzz. Candidates keep asking about what makes us so special. Why do people line up ahead of time to land a job? Funny thing is, we're the same company. The only thing we've changed is how we hire."

Claudia's mindset had also shifted. "Originally, I thought of hiring as an HR function," she said. "Now, I realize the importance of my role. Interviewing candidates before the department has an opening ends up saving time. It also feels less pressured, since I'm not staring across the room at an empty desk."

Always interviewing and occasionally hiring is an important goal in High Velocity Hiring. Once open seats are filled, hiring managers become active participants in lining up prospective employees before they're needed. These potential new hires become part of the company's Talent Inventory. In our next chapter, we'll explore creating Talent Inventories in detail.

Action List for Chapter 6

To implement experiential interviewing, take the following actions.

Rally Your Hiring Team

If you've not yet pulled together your hiring team, now's the time. Already have a hiring team? Set aside time in the coming days to plan how you'll conduct your first experiential interview.

Handle Resistance

You may find that some of your colleagues are hesitant to adopt experiential interviews. That's not uncommon, especially when they've been conducting conventional interviews for years. Suggest a short-term experiment to give experiential interviewing a try. Perhaps, they'd be open to a healthy competition, as in the story of Troy and Claudia.

Create Your Plan

Discuss with your team who will coordinate interview scheduling and communications. Decide on who'll be present at each stage, including who'll facilitate meetings. Be sure to schedule time after each stage to conduct an immediate debrief while candidate details are top of mind. Leverage the expertise of HR or the talent acquisition department as you structure each part of your plan.

Create Launching Questions

Having questions ready ahead of time will allow you to remain fully present during interviews and reference checks. Work with your hiring team to create a handful of initial questions for each stage.

Practice First

Conduct a trial run. You'll be better prepared and more present for the real thing. Preparation also creates a better experience for the candidate, making your company more attractive.

Require Leaders to Always Interview, Occasionally Hire

Fast and accurate hiring is a strategic imperative. A top-down mandate that all hiring managers are always interviewing, occasionally hiring will ensure your company can fill open jobs in an instant.

Step #5—
Maintain a Talent
Inventory

Create a Pool of People
Ready to Hire

Imagine a warehouse stocked with talented people. When you need an administrative assistant, a controller, or a COO, you pick one from the right shelf. They immediately get to work, keeping business moving along.

A people-as-products approach bears a conceptual resemblance to the methods used by retail establishments. Stores plan for demand, stockpile products, manage sales, and refresh their inventories to keep them from becoming depleted.

Stockpiling the talent your company will need is easier than running a store. There are no buildings to erect or expensive inventories to maintain. You won't have to fabricate a product or manage a complex delivery system. Creating a Talent Inventory is a straightforward proposition: You line up people who are ready to hire the moment they're needed.

The Inventory Advantage

For years, I've preferred buying from a locally owned shop. I've enjoyed the opportunity to get to know a store's owner and staff, and support a business right in my backyard. Unfortunately, my desire to shop locally hasn't always worked as I've intended.

Take, for example, the small hardware store six blocks from my home. The products are reasonably priced and the staff is helpful. Do I buy exclusively from this nearby store? No, in fact, when I need something for a project, I'm more apt to drive a mile to the home improvement superstore. Why? My neighborhood store frequently hasn't had what I've needed. My contradictory behavior is a conditioned response: Even though I prefer shopping small, I often buy big, knowing that the superstore will have what I need now.

I'm not alone in how I shop. Companies that can meet our demands immediately prosper. Big-box stores, such as Home Depot, IKEA, and Walmart, attract our business by providing on-the-spot access to thousands of items. On-demand vendors continue to increase their market share as they quickly connect us with their products, such as downloadable music, or services like a ride to the airport the moment we need it.

Companies with immediately accessible inventories keep us invested. Being able to buy something instantly draws us to that store or vendor again and again. We've learned we can rely on them to have what we need in stock, ready to go.

That's the inventory advantage—readily accessible inventories provide shared benefits. Buyers benefit from efficiently getting what they need. Sellers are rewarded for providing value. Other involved parties, such as product manufacturers, artists whose music is downloaded, and drivers for Uber, are paid for what they do.

A ready-to-hire inventory of prospective employees—a Talent Inventory—also provides benefits to everyone involved. Your company has people ready to hire, when they're needed. You're able to focus on doing work instead of being distracted by empty seats. Prospective employees get to line up a better job.

Talent Inventories also provide a strategic benefit. Quality employees are necessary to implement your strategies and serve customers. Organizations without enough talented people are limited on how quickly they can innovate and grow. That's why CEOs are frequently the most fervent advocates of lining up future hires before they're required.

It's been said that knowledge is power. In business, real power is about people. Becoming and remaining a competitive local company, dominant national player, or global powerhouse requires that you constantly have enough people doing quality work. Talent Inventories ensure your organization will have those people when needed.

The Impact of a Talent Inventory

Your Talent Inventory consists of a roster of people ready to be hired. During experiential interviews, you and each person in your inventory have gotten to know one another. You've met them, they've met you and your team, and they've experienced the kind of work they'd do each day. There's mutual attraction—everyone would benefit from working together.

When a job opens, you offer them the role. If they accept, that job is filled. In cases where they don't, you offer it to the next candidate in your inventory. Just like retailers keep shelves stocked to meet buyer needs, you'll maintain at least several prospective employees in your Talent Inventory at all times.

Maintaining an adequate inventory is a cornerstone of High Velocity Hiring, and why the first four steps of the process are vital. Well-crafted hiring profiles clarify who fits a job and guide you in where to find candidates. A continuous flow of candidates provides talented people for you to interview. Your hiring team is always interviewing and occasionally hiring, keeping your Talent Inventory well stocked and ready to go.

Sounds (relatively) simple, right? It is. And it also gives your company a better return on the effort invested in hiring.

The efficiency of the employee selection process can be measured. One way is to look at your return on recruiting (ROR). ROR measures how many hires result from your efforts. You'll likely find that maintaining a Talent Inventory at least doubles the number of quality hires made from the time you invest.

Because of the impact and flexibility of Talent Inventories, they're used in companies of all sizes. How these inventories are built varies, depending on a company's structure and hiring needs.

If you're a manager in a small company, your Talent Inventory will probably be maintained by you. Such an inventory may only center around one or two core roles. An HR manager or office administrator can help you maintain a strong flow of candidates, as well as participate in some of the interviewing stages. Each month, you'll spend a handful of hours making sure you consistently have a few people ready to hire.

If you work in a mid-sized organization, your Talent Inventory will be managed by you and HR. It will likely include all your core roles. The HR team will actively recruit candidates, using all of the eight talent streams. You'll be asked for help with at least two of the talent streams: networking and referrals. HR will help coordinate experiential interviews, and may be part of your hiring team. A few times a month, you'll interview candidates to keep your prospective employee roster active.

Large corporations build Talent Inventories beyond their core roles. If you're a leader in one of these organizations, you'll have help throughout the hiring process from your HR department or talent acquisition team. They'll sustain the flow of talent, asking for your ongoing help with referrals. They may play an active role in each step of experiential interviews, and are likely to share a role in keeping your Talent Inventory candidates interested in your company. You'll meet new candidates monthly, but this will take a fraction of the time compared to the old way of hiring.

Regardless of company size or business type, your Talent Inventory keeps seats filled. If you're like most leaders engaged in the new way of hiring, you'll have less stress, easier workdays, and a more satisfying career. You may even sleep better at night, knowing you have enough people to get work done, with others waiting in the wings.

Accidental Instantaneous Hiring

Change is inevitable, driving the need for new business practices and innovations. For New York HR executive, Beth Casey-Bellone, one thing that hasn't changed for the past 15 years is her use of a Talent Inventory. Casey-Bellone's career has included stints at a global human capital management company and a boutique luxury residential services firm. She's found that regardless of her employer's focus or size, a Talent Inventory has been indispensable in filling jobs quickly.

When I first shared how a Talent Inventory would allow her to fill jobs in an instant, she embraced the concept immediately. "I love having people ready to go," she said. "We always need good candidates and never have enough." Doubt then clouded her face: "I'm not sure that's possible, though. We can't manufacture people. We certainly can't store them in a warehouse—that's called kidnapping!"

She only saw the validity of this approach when I pointed out her team had already done instantaneous hiring, albeit accidentally. "You're right," she said. "We've filled jobs immediately when we happened to be talking with good candidates. We've got to line up more of these good candidates before we need them. What we're missing is a process to make this happenstance a regular occurrence."

Together, we implemented the Talent Accelerator Process. The recruiting team leveraged each talent stream. Recruiters managed the first few steps of the interviewing process, passing on qualified candidates to hiring managers for a hands-on interview. Where there was an open job, hires were made immediately. The remaining candidates became part of a talent-packed "storehouse" of people ready to hire. Casey-Bellone's team shouldered the responsibility for keeping the people in the Talent Inventory engaged until the company could hire them.

Whereas hiring used to take weeks, it quickly dropped to days. Both white- and blue-collar jobs at company sites around the city were filled by high-quality people faster than ever. Before long, many roles were filled the same day, achieving "zero-to-fill," reducing the time it takes to hire to zero.

A decade and a half later, Casey-Bellone still relies on a Talent Inventory. "I've maintained Talent Inventories in each company I've worked," she said. "Having a ready-made group of people available has made my job easier. In my current role, we often need dozens of people with little notice. The only reason we can make that happen is through our Talent Inventory."

Like Casey-Bellone, you've probably experienced accidental, instantaneous hiring. You were in touch with the right person at the right time. Creating a Talent Inventory lets you have these happy "accidents" all the time.

Building Your Talent Inventory

The first four steps of the Talent Accelerator Process feed your Talent Inventory.

The profile you created (Step 1) defines who fits your job and guides you in improving the flow of talent (Step 2). Your hiring team works together to counter hiring blindness (Step 3), conducting interviews (Step 4) to determine if a candidate meets the needs of your company. Candidates that fit are hired immediately or added to your inventory.

Earlier in the book, I asked you to decide how many roles you'll fill instantly. Now's a good time to revisit that decision (or make it if you've not already done so).

I suggested grouping your jobs into these three categories: Core roles, essential roles, and supportive roles.

Core Roles

An open seat creates an immediate and significant negative impact. The nature or amount of work in this role makes it hard to delegate. Filling the job, because of market demand, tends to be difficult.

Essential Roles

A job opening has a negative impact, but is less severe than a core role. The nature or amount of work isn't as hard to delegate, but is still vital to the company. Filling an essential role is challenging, but tends to take no more than a few weeks.

Supportive Roles

Supportive jobs are important; however, openings for these roles have less impact when compared to core and essential jobs. Work is easier to delegate or cover while a replacement is found. Finding qualified candidates to interview for these roles usually takes a matter of days.

Now that you know more about the Talent Accelerator Process, you may want to change which roles fall under each category. For example, you originally could've thought that the role of supervisor was an essential role. Now, you realize that staff can temporarily cover that job for a short time. You move that role to the supportive category.

Once you've categorized your positions, pick a core role. This could be a job for which you currently have no openings, or a position with open seats that need filling. If you elect a job with open seats, you'll initially use the Talent Accelerator Process to fill that job. Then, you'll harness your flow of candidates to build a storehouse of people.

Creating a Talent Inventory for a role happens in three phases (Figure 7.1).

Phase #1: Build

You'll fill your Talent Inventory with candidates you'd like to hire. You'll identify these candidates through experiential interviews.

FIGURE 7.1   **Creating a Talent Inventory**

1   **2**   **3**

Build   **Maintain**   **Fill**

Phase #2: Maintain

How many candidates will you keep on hand? At least two. Usually more. Because you're always interviewing, it's likely that you'll have several candidates to select from at any one time. Managing your relationship with each person will keep some candidates actively available for months.

Phase #3: Fill

When a job opens, you offer it to the person most qualified. If, for any reason, they decline the offer, you reach out to the next best available candidate. Sustaining ongoing interviews refills your hiring pool, ensuring you have people to choose from.

If you want to build a Talent Inventory for additional roles, do so carefully. It's best to wait until you've reached the "Fill" phase before expanding further. As you add roles, you'll likely need help in managing this efficiently. Your hiring team, an assistant, and employees who report to you, along with your HR or talent acquisition department, can help you maintain your Talent Inventory.

Your goal will forever be the same—being able to hire a talented person the moment a job opens. Your Talent Inventory provides you with a pool of ready-to-hire prospective employees, as long as you do your part in keeping it stocked.

Let the Better Salesperson Sell

Hiring is a form of selling: You're selling opportunity. The hope is that the best prospective buyers—top talent—choose you. During interviews, you walk a tightrope, balancing the need to sell the job, while confirming that the candidate is a good fit. Not an easy task when good candidates have many options.

Adding to this challenge is that virtually no one likes to be sold to. We've all been on the receiving end of a sales pitch. It's often an unpleasant experience. Salespeople engage in their own version of the tell, sell, and swell: Telling us why their company is different, selling us on their product's features and benefits, and swelling our egos with compliments. We've learned not to trust everything salespeople say.

If those obstacles weren't enough, there's one more—when you don't have a current job opening. Why would someone who has other job options and doesn't like to be sold to consider waiting for an opportunity?

The Talent Accelerator Process is designed to let the better salesperson sell. That's the candidate, not you. Candidates always believe themselves, but may or may not believe you. If they're going to buy in to your opportunity, they're the best-qualified salespeople to make that happen. Want candidates to believe your company is the best choice? They're the ones who should do the convincing. Will they remain committed to accepting a job in the future? Only if they tell themselves it's the right idea.

How do you get candidates to sell themselves on current or future opportunities at your company? You facilitate a collaborative sales conversation. Collaborative selling lets people play their proper parts. The seller (you) guides the conversation; the buyer (the candidate) does the selling.

To help you engage in collaborative selling as you hire, here are five techniques.

(continued)

Technique #1: Say Little, Ask a Lot

Being frugal with words creates space, allowing the candidates to think and talk. As they talk, they're telling you what they need, why they'd change jobs, and what would make that change worthwhile. Everything they say, they believe. You hear the important details. Ask the right questions, and they could talk themselves into wanting to work for your company.

"Say little, ask a lot" takes practice, especially if your hiring style is a Teller (as noted in Chapter 5). But it's worth it. This act alone creates a positive experience for the candidates. They get to be heard and don't feel like they're on the receiving end of a sales pitch.

Technique #2: Launch and Integrate

Launching questions will help you as you facilitate collaborative sales conversations. For instance, you could ask candidates the following questions in a debrief after a hands-on interview:

- "What do you like most about our company? This opportunity?"

- "How will this job improve your skills? Your career?"

- "Who do you look forward to working with here? Why?"

Their answers can be integrated into additional questions, allowing you to understanding them completely. They'll tell themselves why they should accept a job offer, if one is made. The information uncovered also makes it easier for you to show them why a job fits their specific needs.

Technique #3: Recap and Confirm

During conversations with candidates, it's wise to summarize what you've heard from time to time. Recapping what they've told you has three benefits: You confirm your understanding, you show them that what they say matters, and they hear a summary of their own thoughts and ideas.

(continued)

Technique #4: Let the Better Closer Close

Candidates aren't just the better salespeople—they're also the better closers. If anyone can convince them to say "yes" to a job offer now or later, it's them. Getting them to close themselves on selecting your company requires asking closing questions, such as:

- "If we work together, how can we make it mutually beneficial?"

- "How might our company fit into your future?"

- "How soon would you like to start?"

Technique #5: Continue the Courtship

The professional relationship that begins with the hiring process has to be nurtured and maintained. Especially when candidates are part of your Talent Inventory. Keeping in touch—at least every month—can grow your rapport. Collaborative sales conversations that continue the courtship can include questions like:

- "What's changed since we last spoke?"

- "How can I support you right now?"

Frequently Asked Questions

Answers to ten common questions will help you implement your Talent Inventory.

FAQ #1: How many candidates should I have in my Talent Inventory?

You'll need at least two people for each type of job. Often, you'll have more than two ready to hire at all times. The practice of always interviewing, occasionally hiring will create a growing number of candidate relationships. Some of these relationships will span months. It's common that job offers are made to people whom you've courted for years.

Circumstances at your company will dictate the precise inventory levels you'll need for each role. Periods of rapid growth or high turnover can require that extra candidates for each role be maintained in your inventory.

FAQ #2: How do I get people interested in being part of my Talent Inventory?

People like special treatment. Picture an exclusive nightclub. Outside there are two admission lines—the long line and the shorter one for VIPs. That's the one blocked off by the red velvet rope. Considering someone for your inventory is a red velvet rope experience.

The Talent Accelerator Process allows you to give talented people special treatment. Special access to your company makes people feel important. Experiential interviews are a premium experience, giving the candidate a unique opportunity to experience the job. Collaborative sales conversations will continue the experience, distinguishing you from other companies.

FAQ #3: We don't have any current openings, and I'm not going to lie and say we do. Why, then, would a busy and talented candidate speak with us?

The very fact that you don't have openings is in your favor. There are lots of companies that are always hiring. Their constant churn of people creates the need to fill open seats. Is that where talented people want to work? No. They look for better jobs, and are willing to wait for them.

Cultivating candidates and waiting for the right jobs to open up make your company desirable. It demonstrates that your company is a better place to work, one that's worth waiting for.

FAQ #4: What if our company doesn't have a good reputation? How can we attract top talent for our Talent Inventory?
Organizations are a reflection of their people. A poor reputation happens as a result of the work being done by some of those people. Improving the image of an organization requires upgrading your workers.

High Velocity Hiring builds better companies. How? By hiring your way to a better company. You can use the Talent Accelerator Process to incrementally hire better people. Each round of hiring allows you to fill a job with a better person than the last one.

FAQ #5: What if I don't have HR or talent acquisition staff to help me?
You get to choose the size and scope of your Talent Inventory. Only have time to maintain one role? That's fine. Have time for more? That works too. Talent Inventories are flexible.

In the next chapter, you'll learn methods for keeping your Talent Accelerator Process flowing.

FAQ #6: How do I keep good candidates interested over the long term?
The relationship with each person in your Talent Inventory is a courtship. You're nurturing the growing rapport. The most important thing to remember is it's your job to keep the relationship going.

A simple rule of thumb is to connect with each candidate in your Talent Inventory at least monthly. In a matter of minutes, you can facilitate a meaningful conversation. These conversations maintain the relationship, deepening the candidate's interest in working for your organization.

FAQ #7: I'm an HR or talent acquisition professional. What's my responsibility in maintaining a Talent Inventory?

Often, you and your departmental colleagues will be responsible for harnessing talent through improved candidate gravity. It's also common that you'll coordinate interviews. In some cases, you'll have full responsibility for choosing candidates for hands-on interviews and conducting reference and background checks.

FAQ #8: What if someone in my Talent Inventory turns down a job offer?

It's not *if*, but *when* candidates turn your offers down. The best candidates will have other options.

When someone turns down an offer, you move on to the next best person in your inventory. That's why you're always interviewing, occasionally hiring. Stay in touch at least quarterly with every good candidate who turns your offer down. Things change. You'll want to be there when they do.

FAQ #9: This all sounds very time-consuming. How do I fit this into my schedule?

Doing something different, such as maintaining a Talent Inventory, can seem overwhelming. However, experiential interviews take less time than conventional methods. Staying in touch with the people in your inventory takes minutes. You're likely to find that the total amount of time you spend on hiring is cut at least in half.

Best of all, you're in control. You get to decide how many different roles are in your inventory.

FAQ #10: I'm really busy. Do you really expect me to manage my own Talent Inventory?

Yes. Faster hiring is a strategic imperative. Maintaining an inventory will allow you to fill seats the moment they open. You'll also hire better people and save time while doing it.

Managing a Talent Inventory means different things in different companies. One thing remains the same: Leaders play a vital role in ensuring they have their next hire ready to go.

Talent Inventory Examples

How will you build your Talent Inventory? Who, if anyone, will help you maintain it? How have companies chosen to tackle these tasks? Following are five examples.

Everyone Participates

A global hotelier chose to build an inventory for all their jobs. Managing this inventory became everyone's responsibility. From the top down, every employee has tasks. Executives in the C-Suite facilitate hands-on interviews and personally call each candidate in their inventory each month. Managers in every department do the same, adding phone interviews to their responsibilities. Staff members participate in hands-on interviews, completing scorecards for each candidate. The HR team is responsible for maintaining strong candidate gravity and scheduling interviews.

Everyone in the company has a common, shared responsibility—feeding the referral and networking talent streams.

Divide and Conquer

The CEO of a growing energy company saw one obstacle to future success—people. Numerous departments within the company were struggling to find good people. Anticipated growth was only going to make matters worse. The chief human resource officer was tasked with ensuring the company could fill all jobs the instant they opened.

She divided the talent acquisition team into two groups. The legacy group was responsible for maintaining the Talent Inventory for existing roles. The emergent group built pools of prospective employees for new openings. Both groups worked directly with hiring managers to coordinate the steps of experiential interviews.

Always Elevating

Promoting from within was considered a cultural value of a nonprofit organization. To achieve this, the organization had developed a leadership development program. However, they often lacked people to replace staff members who were ready for promotion. The small HR staff couldn't keep up with the organization's hiring needs, keeping these emerging leaders stuck in their current roles.

A new module was added to the leadership development program called Always Elevating. This module showed participants how to use the Talent Accelerator Process. After completing the program, participants became responsible for helping line up their own replacements.

One Is Enough

Sometimes, filling one type of job on demand is enough. That job, for a small engineering firm, was electrical engineers. When they had enough electrical engineers, they could take on additional projects, adding millions in additional revenue.

Hiring electrical engineers fell on the shoulders of the engineering manager. She was the department's sole leader. The company had an HR director, but she was a part-time employee who was unable to provide any hiring support. The engineering manager sought outside help from a staffing agency. They provided candidates; she conducted interviews, built her Talent Inventory, and kept in touch with those in it. Investing a few hours each month allowed her to maintain an inventory of engineers.

Core Focus

Assemblers were a core role at a mid-sized medical device manufacturer. For months, people in these roles had to work overtime because of unfilled jobs. The extra money was great, for a while. As months went by, people left. Those that remained were at a breaking point, as was the company's budget. Overtime was costing thousands in additional expense—well beyond what had been allocated for the fiscal year.

The company had one recruiter, who was given additional help to fill the open jobs. Once the jobs were filled, he collaborated with the production manager to maintain a Talent Inventory. A handful of assemblers, ready to hire, is all it took to ensure they could always hire in an instant. However, they rarely had to replace someone. Turnover of assemblers had all but been eliminated.

Keeping Your Talent Inventory Full

Talent Inventories aren't foolproof. Sometimes they fail. Why? Hires are made, but the pool of talent isn't replenished. This lack forces you back into the old way of hiring— keeping a job open until the right person shows up. That's why it's critical that you're always interviewing to maintain a pool of people.

Maintaining strong candidate gravity will ensure you have enough candidates to interview. The referral and networking streams can be especially effective in helping you restock your

Talent Inventory as each hire is made. Here are three examples of creative ways to use these talent streams.

BYOC (Bring Your Own Colleague)

Being offered a new job is exciting. You can encourage new hires to share this excitement with friends and colleagues. Ask your new employees to invite people they know to join them at your company. Suggest they bring resumes of their colleagues with them during their first week of employment.

Family Night

The families of your new hires are powerful. They know tons of people, some of whom could be future hires. Invite the families of each new employee to a dinner or reception during the first month of employment. Ask their opinions on whom they know that could be a great addition to your team.

Community Showcase

Have a cool facility? Invented something new? Solved a significant problem? Showing off isn't just okay; it's a great way to get people interested in working for your company. Schedule periodic events to showcase your company and the work you're doing. Partner with community leaders to draw in attendees. Encourage your employees and newest hires to invite friends, family, and colleagues who work at other companies.

Keeping your Talent Inventory full at all times gives your company power. The power of choice. You'll have people to choose from when a job opens. You'll also have immediate options when poor performers need to be replaced. A fully stocked Talent Inventory will be your key to ongoing success, ensuring that you have enough quality people to get work done.

Action List for Chapter 7

Take the following steps to create and maintain your Talent Inventory.

Design Your Warehouse

Will your Talent Inventory cover one role? Two? More? After you've decided how many roles will comprise your Talent Inventory, you'll need a place to "store" your talent. This can be a single sheet of paper, a software database, or an Excel spreadsheet. Whichever you choose, create a separate set of "shelves" for each role. Be sure to include each person's name, telephone, and last contact date. This helps you keep this information at your fingertips.

Set a Deadline

Schedule a deadline for having your Talent Inventory in place. Give yourself a reasonable amount of time. For example, most people need one to two months to build a viable inventory for each role.

Line Up Support

Who, if anyone, will help you build and maintain your Talent Inventory? What's their part? What's yours? Answering these questions will help you plan the implementation of your Talent Inventory.

It's important that each person helping you understand why you have undertaken this initiative. Share Chapter 7 with them, especially the section The Inventory Advantage. This information will help them get up to speed and provide optimum support.

Practice Collaborative Selling

Remember that the Talent Accelerator Process is designed to let the better salesperson sell. That's your candidates, not you. Candidates will always believe themselves, but may or may not believe you. Collaborative selling will help you get candidates to sell themselves on your job opportunities.

Some people believe practice makes perfect. While I've yet to find anyone who's perfect at collaborative selling, you can perfect your skills. Practice each of the collaborative selling techniques mentioned earlier in this chapter with a colleague. Keep at it until you demonstrate proficiency in letting candidates do the selling.

Share Your Success

Success breeds further success. Share your wins in building your Talent Inventory with your colleagues. Show them how you did it, and what you learned along the way. Remember that teaching skills to others will deepen your own.

Plan for Replenishment

How will you replenish your Talent Inventory? Will you schedule a community showcase, family night, or invite new hires to BYOC (bring their own colleagues)? Maybe all three? What other creative ways can you use candidate gravity to ensure you have people to interview? By planning now how you'll refill your Talent Inventory, you're likely to have the candidates you need, when you need them.

Measure Efficiency

Keeping your TAP functioning efficiently will help you maintain a full Talent Inventory. How will you know if your TAP is working properly? Here are three indicators to keep an eye on.

- **Zero-to-Fill:** The goal of High Velocity Hiring is filling jobs with quality people in an instant. When you're filling jobs the same day they open, you've reduced time-to-fill to zero. This is called zero-to-fill. It takes zero days to fill jobs covered by your Talent Inventory. At the end of the day, you have none of those jobs left to fill.

  As you build your Talent Inventory, you'll want to monitor time-to-fill. That number should steadily decrease. Once you reach and maintain zero-to-fill, you'll know your TAP is operating efficiently. Keep monitoring the zero-to-fill status for each role in the inventory. If this number begins to inch above zero, take immediate action to find and address where your TAP is starting to break down.

- **Return on Recruiting (ROR):** ROR measures how many hires result from your efforts. The more you use your Talent Accelerator Process, the less effort it should take to hire new employees. ROR will help you monitor your progress.

  Each month, you'll add up time spent on hiring and divide that by the number of hires made. You'll include everyone involved in the steps of your Talent Accelerator Process when tallying time—your hiring team, HR, and talent acquisition staff. By tracking this each month, you'll know if your ROR improves, declines, or stays the same.

  For example, let's say you made 10 hires this month and that this took 60 total hours. Dividing 60 hours by 10 hires gives you an ROR of one hire for every six hours invested. The following month you make 12 hires in a total of 58 hours. That's an ROR of one hire every 4.8 hours, an improvement over the previous month.

What's a reasonable ROR goal? This varies among different types of organizations. Some have achieved an impressive ROR of one hire for every three hours invested for staff roles and one hire for every four hours invested for leadership roles.

- **New-Hire Churn:** What percentage of your new hires leave or are terminated in the first 90 days? The first six months? The first year? Check this percentage at each interval. Companies maintaining Talent Inventories have reduced yearly churn to less than 1 percent.

Step #6—
Keep the TAP Flowing

Ensure Hiring Can Always
Be Done in an Instant

The Talent Accelerator Process (TAP) is like a hiring machine. Once set up, TAP delivers employees on-demand. Jobs stay filled. Work gets done. In a perfect world, this hiring machine would never break. It would always generate a flow of quality talent, keeping your seats filled with good employees.

Does TAP ever break down? It does. Any machine that isn't properly used will eventually fail. If the flow of prospective employees from your TAP slows, the cause will always be the same—people. Someone, maybe even you, didn't maintain the TAP. Could be that you overlooked an important Dealbreaker and hired someone who wasn't a good fit. Maybe you relied on one or two talent streams instead of using all eight. Possibly, you reverted back to conceptual interviewing, allowing a candidate to tell, sell, and swell their way into a job. Each step of TAP is important. Skipping one step creates a domino effect, causing the entire system to fail.

Why does this happen? Why would anyone take the time to build something and then fail to use it properly? The answer is simple: We're human. We're fallible creatures. We create complicated plans, forget to do what's important, and make costly mistakes.

This is why good strategies fail. People fail the strategy.

Watching your plans unravel is frustrating. Especially when your plans deal with something as crucial as hiring. This chapter is dedicated to helping you avoid this frustration. We'll explore how you and your colleagues could cause your TAP to fail inadvertently. You'll gain ideas to keep this from happening, allowing you to get the most from the new way of hiring.

That strategic initiatives fail isn't unique to hiring. Our human nature is the root cause of strategic failures, which is why the ideas presented in the coming pages are important. When applied to all of your strategies, the more likely those strategies will succeed as well.

The Failure Factors

How do people cause plans to fail? These four factors are the most common.

Failure Factor #1: We Complicate What's Simple

Every year, I chuckle when I look at the latest tax form from the U.S. Internal Revenue Service. The bottom of Form 1040 makes reference to the "Paperwork Reduction Act." This must be a bad joke, the kind told by a bureaucrat. My tax return grows a few pages each year.

If the Paperwork Reduction Act is real, it's not working. On the contrary, U.S. tax laws have continued to grow in length and complexity. Totaling over seven million words, the tax code has more than doubled in size since 1985.[1]

Look beyond governments and you'll find many examples of needless complexity. Computer instruction manuals are convoluted. Blueprints for assembling furniture don't make sense. Employee handbooks are filled with confusing jargon.

We're good at making things complicated. When one page of instructions will do, we'll write two. If a process takes three steps, we'll expand it to four. We're smart creatures, sometimes too smart. Unfortunately, our intellect can frustrate others, irritating them to the point of giving up. Sometimes it's easier to throw in the towel.

We complicate what's simple. It's the first of the four failure factors. These factors undermine sound strategies, disrupting our well-made plans. They're the primary reason why proven methods, like the Talent Accelerator Process, fail. Left unchecked, one or more of the failure factors will eventually slow your fast hiring.

Failure Factor #2: We're Easily Distracted

There are lots of things vying for our attention: The ringing phone, all those emails, the meeting you need to prepare for, a text from your spouse.

When we're distracted, we forget what's most important. We answer the phone, learning the call was about something mundane. We react to each email as it arrives, forgetting that most messages don't require immediate attention.

Distractions keep us from important tasks. They also undermine our focus when doing vital work. How many times have you been on the phone while checking email and sifting through a stack of documents?

Just like distracted driving causes car accidents, working while distracted creates work mishaps. We miss details, forget things, and make mistakes.

Failure Factor #3: We Change Too Much at Once

Patience may be a virtue, one that many of us lack. In today's fast-paced society, impatience is the norm. We want things done now, not weeks from now. To drive change, we often set tight deadlines and push everyone, including ourselves, toward the goal.

The problem is that fast change doesn't stick. It takes time to adjust our routines and change our habits. A rapid series of changes overwhelms us. When our sense of being overwhelmed reaches a tipping point, we give up and revert back to our previous routines.

Failure Factor #4: Our Intentions Don't Become Actions

How many times have your intentions failed? You intended to eat better, but it didn't happen. You meant to work out, but your gym bag lies untouched on the office floor.

The good news is you're not alone. Everyone fails at least some of the time in turning intentions into actions. The bad news is that the disconnect between intentions and actions causes strategic failure. For goals to be realized, like being able to fill your core roles in an instant, you and your colleagues must keep taking action. Not just intend to take action.

Unless you counter the failure factors, they'll end up running the show. As human nature kicks in, your colleagues will complicate how they conduct experiential interviews. The desire to fill all of your jobs in an instant will prompt you to take on too many at once. Distractions will cause your staff to overlook interview warning signs. The candidates in your Talent Inventory will be lost to other employers when your intention to stay in touch doesn't equate to action.

This sixth and final step of the Talent Accelerator Process will counteract the failure factors. Four countermeasures will help you eliminate their negative effects, ensuring that your TAP remains a well-oiled hiring machine.

Countering Failure Factor #1: Keep It Swift and Simple

To fill jobs, a UK-based retailer used to take months. One position in particular, the buyer role, was especially hard to fill. The company looked for people with previous experience as a retail buyer. However, many candidates lacked this background.

The retailer decided to give TAP a try. They created a Hire-Right Profile, adding several transferable skills as Dealmakers. This allowed the talent acquisition team to draw in additional candidates for experiential interviews. Open seats were filled quickly and a surplus of talent was lined up.

The success in filling buyer jobs prompted the retailer to expand the use of TAP. Roles in the accounting department were added next, followed by key positions in marketing and retail management. In less than a year, they'd reduced time-to-fill for these key positions to zero. They'd also built a Talent Inventory for nine core roles.

Wrapping up our work together, I offered the following advice: "Remember that simple is sustainable. If you make changes to your TAP, be sure that those changes keep the hiring process swift and simple."

Six months later, the retailer called me in a panic. The Talent Inventory for most of the core roles had been depleted. Filling these jobs went from minutes to weeks. Hiring managers and recruiters were working harder than ever to fill them.

What was the problem? The TAP had become bloated. Dozens of additional criteria had been added to Hire-Right Profiles. Hands-on interviews were taking four hours. The number of questions asked in reference checks had doubled.

It's normal, even preferable, that you'll fine-tune your TAP over time. However, the staff at this retailer had gone too far. Instead of carefully considering changes to the process, "improvements" were automatically adopted.

The retailer had quickly forgotten that simple is sustainable. As the complexity of the TAP grew, the harder it was to maintain. Interviewers were overwhelmed by the expanded Hire-Right Profiles and ended up missing details during interviews. Longer interviews and lengthy reference checks also meant less time was available to recruit new candidates. Undoing the damage to the TAP wasn't easy. A complete reset of the system was required, rebuilding TAP one role at a time.

When asked what they'd learned from this experience, the retailer mentioned two things. "First," they said, "rebuilding our Talent Accelerator Process was worth the effort. Being able to fill our core jobs the instant they open made us more competitive. Second, screwing up our TAP was optional. Had we followed the instructions—Keep It Swift and Simple—we wouldn't have had to start over."

Like this retailer, you'll gain important insights as you use your Talent Accelerator Process. These insights can improve the process, if applied in the right way.

What's the right way? Do the four things that are mentioned next.

Action #1: Put Someone in Charge

Designate someone the TAP Lead, the person responsible for overseeing your Talent Accelerator Process. This could be you, a department manager, an HR director, or a senior recruiter. Whomever you choose, they are responsible for monitoring the TAP. Changes, such as adding criteria to the Hire-Right Profile or adding a question to phone interviews, are facilitated by the TAP Lead. They bring those proposed changes to your hiring team for review.

Action #2: Discuss the Change

The hiring team considers each change, asking questions like:

- "How will it increase the effectiveness of our TAP?"

- "Will the change maintain or improve hiring speed?"

- "Is it simple, so we can easily repeat it each time we hire?"

The hiring team should approve only simple changes that keep your TAP swift and efficient.

Action #3: Implement the Change

The TAP Lead is responsible for implementing the change, updating documentation as needed.

Action #4: Monitor the Impact

Did the change have the desired impact? Is your TAP still operating effectively? The TAP Lead keeps an eye on improvements, answering these questions for each. Any issues are immediately brought to the attention of the hiring team for their help in resolving them.

Countering Failure Factor #2: Reduce Multitasking

The success of Andrea's business hinged on having good account managers. They were the face of her travel company, the first line of contact for customers. For over a year, she'd been five account managers short. The rest of the team had to pick up the slack, creating a larger workload for everyone. Mistakes were made, accounts were neglected, and some customers took their business elsewhere.

Andrea and her company had been engaged in the old way of hiring for two decades. She knew it was time to do something different. When she heard about being able to hire in an instant, she loved the idea.

The next few months were spent implementing the Talent Accelerator Process. To keep things simple, Andrea decided that the only core role would be account managers. The company followed the steps in order, using their TAP to fill open seats and then build a Talent Inventory.

For three years, TAP kept time-to-fill to zero. If Andrea needed an additional account manager, she hired one that same day. When someone resigned, that position was filled in an instant. Turnover was virtually zero. Running the company had become easier than ever, and business was flourishing.

The good times allowed Andrea to invest some of the profits. New computers, upgraded software, and a state-of-the-art phone system were installed. Now, account managers could manage larger books of business in less time. Everything seemed to be going right. Andrea started making plans for expansion, including the possibility of acquiring one of her biggest competitors.

This long run of success came to a halt a few months later. The problems were subtle at first. A few of the talent streams that had been drawing in great candidates seemed to dry up. Then, there was a series of bad hires, people who turned out to be a poor fit for the account manager job. Before long, the Talent Inventory became dangerously depleted.

Where had they gone wrong? It began when they upgraded their technology. The improvements themselves, however, weren't the issue. How they used those tools was.

Instead of making work efficient, technology ushered in an increase in multitasking. Everyone was trying to juggle too much at once. They'd be on the phone, entering details into the new software, watching for emails, and peeking at their instant messenger window—all at the same time. Distractions were also affecting hiring. Interviewers were responding to emails during phone interviews instead of giving the conversation their undivided attention. Working while distracted was also causing people to forget important tasks, including maintaining strong candidate gravity.

Solving this problem was straightforward. Distracted work had become the habit, and multitasking fed that habit. Andrea had to reduce multitasking. Changing this behavior would require more than implementing new policies. She had to shake things up.

Andrea called the company together for a meeting. Like an alcoholic in a 12-step group, she stood up and said, "Hi, my name is Andrea and I'm addicted to multitasking." Her team shifted in their seats, looked confused, and said nothing. Andrea shared how she'd become hooked on multitasking. She admitted it was interfering with her work, and confessed that she was even multitasking in interviews. The longer she continued, the more she saw heads nod.

In wrapping up, she invited others to "come clean." Her vulnerability had paved the way, as a dozen people took turns in front of the room. Their stories had the same theme: Doing too much at once had become the norm. Each person admitted they were distracted, making mistakes, and forgetting important tasks.

Andrea proposed a solution—"single-tasking"—a way of staying focused on one responsibility when that responsibility was of vital importance. She explained what she considered important. Included on her list were reviewing resumes, interviews with job candidates, and conversations with customers. Andrea asked everyone to join her in the practice of single-tasking.

Single-tasking got hiring back on track. The Talent Inventory was replenished and the quality of hires improved. But that was only the start. Single-tasking positively affected all aspects of the business. Employees were happier. Customer satisfaction scores increased. Revenues grew to all-time highs.

Am I suggesting that your company eliminate multitasking completely? No. I don't believe that's possible in today's work world. What I'm recommending is that you limit distractions, especially when it comes to important tasks. Choosing the right people for your organization is that important. It can make or break you.

If something is important, it deserves our full attention. Single-tasking lets you devote that attention.

Countering Failure Factor #3: Promote Incremental Change

Success is infectious. The more success we have, the more of it we want. Sometimes, our successes can deceive us, prompting decisions we later regret.

My biggest mistake in using the Talent Accelerator Process came from such a success. I'd reduced time-to-fill for every position in our corporate office to zero. Our entire management team was on board, happily practicing our mantra of always interviewing, occasionally hiring. The Talent Inventory was stocked with good people.

I took this as a sign that we were ready. I thought we should expand our use of the Talent Accelerator Process to our branch offices. I came up with an aggressive timeline for rolling out TAP to ten of these offices over the next 30 days.

Given the size of this initiative, I needed help. I pulled together my team and presented "TAP in a Box," my name for the rollout. I explained that over the coming weeks we were going to visit each of the ten offices. We'd show them how to implement TAP, leaving behind a box of reference materials. Then, we'd host monthly conference calls to measure progress and answer questions.

I still remember my team members' surprised looks, especially when I shared the rollout schedule. They questioned the short timeline. Some openly expressed their doubts we'd succeed.

In the end, I won. I was the boss. We hopped on planes and held meetings in each office. TAP in a Box was met with enthusiasm, further fueling my belief that I was doing the right thing. Best of all, we completed the rollout in our 30-day window.

The next few months went poorly. Our branch offices were struggling to incorporate the steps of TAP into their calendars. Time-to-fill increased for the core roles in their Talent Inventories. My team was overwhelmed with calls and questions by email. Monthly conferences calls for the initiative became complaint sessions.

After three months, I had to admit I was wrong. I'd pushed too fast and too hard. My intent was honorable: I wanted our branches to benefit from TAP. However, my impatience under-mined my good intentions.

Looking back decades later, it's easy to see where I went wrong. Yet, in the moment, it wasn't so easy. I fell into the success trap, believing that success always begets more success. What I failed to realize, at the time, is this happens only if you have a process in place to effectively leverage that success.

My greatest lesson from this rushed implementation was the value of incremental change. To be effective, change can never outpace your ability to adjust habits and routines. Incremental change eliminates feeling overwhelmed.

It's likely you'll never blunder to the degree I did as you imple-ment TAP. However, it's normal that some level of impatience, your own or others', will hamper your efforts. To avoid this, I suggest you follow one important rule: Mind the gap.

When riding a train, we're told to mind the gap, that space between the train car and the platform. Minding the gap keeps us safe. With TAP, there's also a gap: It can only fill those jobs for which it was built. Stay mindful of the current capabilities of your TAP. Remember that it takes time to build capacity to fill a role the instant it becomes open. Until you do, that's the gap.

Countering Failure Factor #4: Improve Accountability

In the March 2015 issue of the *Harvard Business Review*, Donald Sull, a senior lecturer at MIT's Sloan School of Management, shared his research on strategy execution: Of the 8,000 manag-ers he surveyed, 84 percent said that the people in their chain of command can be relied upon. However, 59 percent of the managers said that colleagues in other departments couldn't be relied upon.[2]

Sull's research illustrates why our plans fail—strategic initiatives are never solo acts. Improved hiring requires coordinated action and consistent follow-through. Once you implement your TAP, everyone involved must keep doing their part.

Why don't people do what they're supposed to do? The implementation of TAP at a government agency is a classic example. The agency director wanted department heads to hire faster. TAP was his solution. He tasked a project team of recruiters and managers to make this happen.

The project team followed the steps, putting TAP in place in a few months. With great fanfare, the director announced the initiative with a launch event. He explained why faster hiring was important and how TAP would make that happen. Other leaders followed, carefully explaining expectations and answering audience questions. Documents explaining important details, such as how to conduct experiential interviews, were handed out.

The agency director closed the meeting with these words: "I know that change isn't easy or convenient. We've failed at change in the past. But keeping our jobs filled has to happen. We're all adults, so let's each do our part. Let's get this done."

Did the agency get it done? Sort of. Sometimes hires were made quickly; other times they weren't. Inconsistency was the name of the game. Why did this happen? Not everyone followed through. A recruiter had forgotten to maintain a talent stream. A department head neglected to schedule an interview. Failing to follow through hadn't been intentional, but it was still happening and interfering with the goal of faster hiring.

Even though there was no ill intent, it did little to placate the agency director. Sitting in his office, I listened as he ranted about these failures. "Heads need to roll," he said, "I need people I can rely upon."

During his tirade, I'd noticed that on his desk was a big bottle of vitamins. On a hunch, I said, "What if the problem wasn't the people in their roles?" He asked what I getting at. "I noticed that bottle of vitamins," I said. "Why is it there?" He explained that he'd had a heart attack, nearly dying. His doctor had prescribed the vitamins as part of his daily regimen to prevent future heart problems. "Do you always take it daily," I asked? He paused and grudgingly admitted he occasionally forgot; thus the reason it was sitting in such a prominent spot. "I intend to take them because my life depends on it," he said, "but it doesn't always happen."

Our conversation illustrated how intentions can fail to become actions. Here was a guy whose life depended on doing something as simple as taking vitamins. Yet, his intention wasn't enough to make it happen.

I picked up the bottle and asked him to look at its label. "The solution to poor follow-through in this agency is on that bottle." The label mentioned "minimum daily requirements." These were the prescribed amounts of vitamins and minerals necessary to stay healthy. "Just because someone is an adult doesn't mean they'll automatically follow through," I said. "Inconsistent follow-through is part of human nature. Even in life and death situations. People need reminders. They need minimum daily requirements when it comes to specific activities. Instead of intending to do the right thing, the minimum daily requirements spell out exactly what that means."

The agency director had the TAP project team establish minimum daily requirements (MDRs) for hiring. They apportioned tasks into manageable daily (and sometimes weekly) activities. For recruiters, this included daily maintenance of their assigned talent streams. Hiring managers had their own set of MDRs, including interviewing at least one candidate every week. Checklists made it easy for them to stay on track and for department heads to confirm who did their part, and who did not.

Establishing minimum daily requirements will help you ensure that intentions become actions. Every person involved with your Talent Accelerator Process, including you, should have their own set of MDRs. Keep them simple, spelling out what must be done daily, weekly, and monthly. Most important, help one another by serving as accountability partners. Like a spouse who asks if you've remembered to take your vitamins, you and your colleagues can help each other stay on track.

Nice Person Syndrome

Ever heard the statement "Nice guys finish last?" It turns out to be true when it comes to leadership roles.

Succeeding in business requires some degree of niceness and getting along with others. In staff level positions, being nice helps build customer relationships. A collegial attitude also makes it easier to work with colleagues and remain on the boss' good side.

When we're promoted to a leadership role, being nice works against us. Holding employees accountable doesn't feel good. It can make us uncomfortable, even fearful that we won't be liked or that the employee may quit. Sometimes, having to manage people may seem parental, making our jobs unpleasant and exhausting.

What happens when we feel uncomfortable? We hold back. Instead of requiring direct reports to meet standards consistently, we fail to follow through. When employees do shoddy work, we make excuses. If it's time for a reprimand, we delay and hope things will improve on their own.

(continued)

This is Nice Person Syndrome (NPS). NPS enables poor work behaviors, reinforcing the disconnect between intentions and actions. It's why many leaders fail—their niceness gets in the way of keeping their teams on track. NPS is a frequent contributor when a Talent Accelerator Process breaks down.

Do you have NPS? Many leaders do. While the severity of NPS varies by person, a mild case of it hampers effective leadership. To determine if you have NPS, answer four questions:

1. Do you hold your direct reports accountable, no matter what?

2. Do you avoid making excuses when staff members fail to meet expectations?

3. Do you promptly reprimand someone who needs it?

4. Do you swiftly terminate an employee when it's time to let them go?

If you answer "no" to any of these questions, you have NPS. The more frequently you answer "no," the more severe the problem.

Is NPS curable? Not completely. You can, however, keep NPS in remission if you do these three things:

1. **Recognize that accountability is an act of compassion.**

   When you fail to hold others accountable, you're culpable. By doing your part, you help employees stay on track and succeed. When you're tempted to hold back on accountability, remind yourself of the consequences. The discomfort you feel is better than the alternative—having to eventually fire someone in whose demise you played a part.

2. **Remember you're not responsible for your first thought.**

   As someone with NPS, my first thought when having to hold someone to task is usually "yuck." I don't

(continued)

enjoy having to call someone out and doubt this will ever change. I've come to expect this first thought. Instead of ruminating on it, I focus on my next action, which is to be the leader I need to be. You too are not responsible for your first thought, only your next action.

3. **Say what you mean, just don't say it mean.**

   Many leaders dislike conflict, viewing accountability as a potentially difficult conversation. Accountability doesn't have to be harsh. We can express our concerns with kindness. We can say exactly what we need to say without allowing our words to do harm.

The Ultimate Countermeasure

It's likely that your TAP won't function perfectly. Someone will complicate the process, get distracted, make changes too quickly, or fail to follow through. It happens. By planning for when, not if, this occurs, you'll be ready to quickly get hiring back on track.

Do all TAPs slow or break down? No. Like a well-oiled machine that runs for decades, some companies have a TAP that has never failed. What's their secret? They've consistently deployed the ultimate countermeasure: They keep doing the next right thing. No matter what.

When a big project seems of greater importance than maintaining their TAP, they still take time to maintain it. If schedules become overloaded and they're tempted to push aside their minimum daily requirements, they don't. They keep doing the next right thing. One day at a time.

I know this sounds simple. It is simple, as long as we remember that our human nature is to complicate. When it comes down to it, we're capable of doing the next right thing. We need to ask ourselves what that is, and then do it.

The best way to solve a problem is to keep it from happening. Once set up, you can keep your TAP flowing by requiring everyone, including yourself, to keep doing the next right thing. That includes countering the four failure factors the moment one of them arises.

Action List for Chapter 8

The following actions will help you keep your TAP flowing from the start.

Find Your Failure Factors

We repeat our mistakes until we learn from them and change our ways. The mistakes your organization has made in executing strategic plans will show up again and again—unless you keep history from repeating itself.

Review strategies that have failed in the last five years. Which of the four failure factors contributed to these problems? These same issues are the ones most likely to derail your Talent Accelerator Process.

Share the Patterns

Understanding a problem helps us solve it. It's important that everyone involved with TAP understand which failure factors have contributed to previous strategic failures. Share what you've learned from reviewing past mistakes. Provide them with details on the countermeasures in this chapter. Discuss how these can be applied in your circumstances.

Select a TAP Lead Early

Choose a TAP Lead as soon as possible. Ideally, this happens before you begin implementing TAP. This allows TAP Leads to play a role in the rollout and improves their knowledge of the process.

Who should you choose? The skills of the individual matter more than titles. Pick someone who's good with details and has better than average follow-through.

Give Single-Tasking a Try

Experiment with single-tasking. Pick an important task, such as reviewing resumes or conducting a phone interview. Make it your singular focus until done. Notice how this allows you to be present and focused. Pay attention to how single-tasking impacts the quality of your work and the speed with which you get it done. Then, share your experience with your team and ask them to give single-tasking a try. The benefits of incorporating single-tasking into your day can positively affect more than hiring.

Phase in MDRs

When used correctly, minimum daily requirements (MDRs) take the work of hiring and break it down into manageable portions of daily and weekly work. For example, the MDRs of a hiring manager might look like this:

Daily: Review three resumes of prospective candidates.

Weekly: Interview one candidate, check in with two people on the Talent Inventory, ask two people for candidate referrals.

Don't try to implement all your MDRs at once. If you do, the third failure factor, changing too much at once, may negate your work. Phase them in one at a time. As each becomes part of your routine, add the next. And then the next.

Acknowledge Nice Person Syndrome

It's tough for some people to admit that being a nice person has hurt their leadership. Have conversations with your colleagues about Nice Person Syndrome (NPS). Go first to be the one who openly admits how NPS has affected you. Your vulnerability may encourage others to acknowledge this issue in themselves. As part of your conversation, discuss how you can support one another in countering NPS.

Incorporate These Ideas Into Other Strategies

The four failure factors can disrupt any strategic initiative. The countermeasures will keep your initiatives on track.

Lean Recruiting

Deploy Automation to Enhance the Efficiency of Your TAP

Automation helps us make smarter choices and be productive. Take, for example, innovations in the automotive industry. Cars can now warn us of oncoming traffic when we're changing lanes. There are cameras and sensors to help us when we're backing up. If we're poor parallel parkers, some vehicles can park themselves. Certain models will automatically slam on the brakes to keep us from crashing.

The risk with this technology is that we become overreliant on it. When we rely too much on automation, our skills become rusty and our senses dull. Such was the case when a semitrailer pulled in front of a car with autopilot. The autopilot failed to avert an accident. The driver didn't react in time, losing his life in the collision.

Automation isn't perfect. It's created by fallible people and used in imperfect ways.

That's why hiring technology also has its pros and cons. It, too, isn't perfect, nor is it perfectly used. On the one hand, it makes some aspects of hiring more efficient (digital candidate information is paperless and searchable). On the other hand, it creates effort and undesirable outcomes; for example, job boards can flood you with the resumes of hundreds of unusable candidates.

High Velocity Hiring is, by its very nature, lean and efficient. As you build and maintain your Talent Accelerator Process, you'll have ongoing opportunities to improve what you've created. Automation can play an important role in these improvements as long as they keep your hiring methods lean.

The principles of Lean Recruiting will guide you in making smart technological choices. In this chapter, you'll learn about Lean Recruiting. We'll cover how to use it to keep your Talent Accelerator Process running efficiently. You'll also see examples of how organizations have used the three principles of Lean Recruiting to select software, job boards, and other types of automation.

Available technologies change and grow by the day, as do the needs of those who use them. Because of this, I won't be recommending one vendor over another. High Velocity Hiring is agnostic as long as the technology contributes to Lean Recruiting. Instead, I'm going to equip you with methods to avoid common pitfalls and make the right choices when selecting automation.

Technology Myths

Before diving into the practice of Lean Recruiting, we need to address some common myths. Buying into these falsehoods can contribute to poor technology choices.

Myth #1: Technology is More Effective Than Traditional Methods

Nick loves technology. He's got the newest Smartphone, a voice-activated music system, automated grocery ordering, and a state-of-the-art GPS in his car. The GPS comes in especially handy as he travels. His job as a purchasing manager has him constantly on the road, visiting vendors and the 16 locations of the distribution company where he works.

Because he loves technology, Nick's always been ready to try something new. When corporate decided to experiment with video interviewing, he was first in line.

The idea seemed simple. His organization had contracted with an outside vendor for their video interviewing services. Instead of candidates having to come into an office for an interview, it could be done virtually. Candidates would answer interview questions via webcam. The video interviewing service recorded the interviews. Hiring managers would then watch these at their leisure. No one had to travel.

For a road warrior like Nick, this technological setup seemed ideal. He was an effective interviewer, but scheduling was a constant struggle. He never knew more than a day or two ahead where he'd be next. This made scheduling a problem, especially coordinating calendars with other interviewers. Delays in getting interviews scheduled resulted in losing good talent. Nick was tired of losing candidates to competitors, and was hopeful that video interviewing would eliminate this problem.

With great anticipation, he sat down to review his first batch of video interviews. It got off to a rough start. The first two candidates seemed to struggle with the technology. Others seemed to have good skills, but were robotic in how they communicated on their videos. A few candidates seemed promising, prompting Nick to think of questions he'd like to ask. But, he couldn't do that on the spot. By the end of his review, Nick was frustrated but not deterred. As an early adopter of technology, he knew there'd be issues. He was still convinced that video interviews were going to make hiring better.

Over the next few weeks, Nick got used to this different way of assessing talent. He'd had more first "interviews" than ever. In a few days, he'd reviewed a dozen candidates.

Nick sat down with his colleagues, who'd also reviewed the video interviews of these candidates, to compare notes. They'd always been able to make swift decisions after a round of interviews. His hope was they'd decide which candidates to pursue further by the end of their conversation.

That didn't happen. Opinions were all over the place. When one interviewer thought a candidate was a great fit, another interviewer didn't agree. If someone believed a candidate communicated well, someone else differed. Nick was stunned. Never had this group viewed candidates so differently.

Nick quickly spotted the problem as he dug into the details of his colleagues' experiences. Video interviewing may have sped up the first round of interviews, but it interfered with the quality of their selection process. The video format didn't allow them to connect and converse with a candidate. The interviewers struggled to make an honest assessment of which ones could be a fit.

Was video interviewing to blame? No. Nick's peers in other companies were having success with this method. He came to realize that this approach didn't fit his needs. Nor did it solve the real problem—scheduling. Nick revamped his schedule so he could go back to doing in-person interviews.

The Reality

Is technology more effective than traditional methods? Not always. Technology can solve problems, but only when it's the appropriate solution for the problem.

Myth #2: Technology Solves Process Problems

One of my jobs as a consultant is to spot patterns. Patterns are like neon flashing lights that indicate something important. These indicators often point toward persistent problems.

In 2005, I began noticing a pattern. Organizations were rapidly adopting new hiring technologies, and then swiftly abandoning them. It wasn't just one type of technology being tossed aside. Applicant tracking systems, resume parsing software (automated extraction of data from resumes), job boards, online skills testing—all were being treated as disposable.

This pattern caught my attention for three reasons: The prevalence of the behavior, the timing, and the cost. It wasn't happening in a few companies. This was occurring at hundreds of them. They were adopting and discarding their newfound automations within a few months. These organizations had also spent lots of money on these technologies. Yet, they were acting as if this didn't matter.

I set out to understand what was going on. I met with organizations that were engaging in this behavior. Specifically, I looked into their reasons for the quick change of heart. These organizations varied in size, were in a wide range of industries, and were located throughout the world. I wanted to determine if size, industry, or location were factors affecting the pattern.

After five years, I'd met with leaders in 800 organizations. What did I find? Two answers emerged as to why they let go of recently purchased technology so quickly:

- 3 percent of the organizations had been sold a bill of goods.

  The vendors had misrepresented their offering. Once the organizations learned this, they stopped using the technology.

- 97 percent of the organizations had adopted technology for the wrong reason.

  These organizations had tried to use technology to solve hiring process problems. When the technology didn't solve the problem, it got the blame.

  Here's a common example: Hiring managers in some of these organizations were rejecting lots of candidates. To solve the problem, these organizations implemented online skills testing. When this didn't solve the problem, they stopped using it. Was online skills testing to blame? No. The real issue was hiring profiles. They were inaccurate or they weren't being used at all.

The Reality

Can technology fix process problems? No. Not ever. Technology is a tool. In order for technology to work, it has to be part of a well-planned hiring process.

Myth #3: You Must Have the Latest, Greatest Technologies

A construction company in South America has used the same talent management system (TMS) for eight years. The software helps them handle all aspects of hiring and managing employees. They chose their software package because it looked like it would get the job done. It wasn't sophisticated. It had all the functions they needed. Nothing more.

The TMS was a huge hit. They had a well-designed hiring process, and the software fit that process. It reduced data entry, eliminated lots of paper, and tracked candidates throughout the hiring process. When candidates were hired, the TMS also helped the company manage functions like payroll, performance reviews, and storing electronic versions of employee documents.

Has the company ever considered replacing the system? Yes, every year. The human resource executive in charge of the system regularly reviews new offerings. She's called on by a growing number of salespeople each year. "I keep gaining options," she said. "And I keep saying no."

Saying "no" doesn't mean she hasn't come close to making a change. She has. Her current software vendor offered a new product at a substantial discount. Other competing companies have wined her, dined her, and conducted lots of software demos. She takes these demos seriously. "I'm open to something better," she said. "But it has to be substantially better for me to put our people through such a big change. Software conversions are expensive and time consuming."

Once, she got close. A software vendor came to her with a TMS that was getting rave reviews. Some of these were from other construction firms. "I gave that software a close look. It was promising, especially since people in our business seemed to love it."

Her department set up a test run, managing a limited set of data on the new system while maintaining the current one. The new TMS came with innovative features. Lots of them. These were supposed to make the various tasks involved in hiring and managing employees quicker and easier.

After the test, she decided to stick with her company's current system. "Yes, the new TMS we tested had lots of bells and whistles," she said. "And it did increase the efficiency of some aspects of our process. But only slightly so. Our current software may be like an old jalopy, but it gets us where we're going each day."

The Reality

Do you need the latest, greatest hiring technologies to be successful? Not necessarily. Old does not mean obsolete. Sometimes, replacing older technology makes sense. Other times it does not.

Automation makes hiring better, but only if automation is chosen for the right reasons. Companies that buy into myths are likely to make choices they'll later regret. To help you avoid poor choices, let's now look at how the principles of Lean Recruiting can guide you when choosing technology.

The Principles of Lean Recruiting

Hiring is an investment—an investment of time and money. If you're like most people, you don't have time to spare; and you don't want to waste money.

Lean Recruiting is the practice of using automation to make hiring more efficient. The principles of Lean Recruiting (Figure 9.1) set the standard for what automation should do for you. Each of the principles will guide you in making informed decisions when choosing which automations to adopt or discard, helping you get the most from your investment of time and money.

Principle #1: Automation Must Reduce Effort

The primary purpose of automation is to create an automatic means for getting something done. For automation to be effective, it has to reduce our involvement in tasks. When it doesn't, we end up serving our technology instead of it serving us.

FIGURE 9.1 **The Three Principles of Lean Recruiting**

Principle #2: Automation Must Be Easy to Use

Using automation can't be a struggle. This begins with training. A challenging learning curve is overwhelming, causing you to miss important details. If using the technology is difficult, you'll forget to take advantage of key features. When these difficulties persist, you'll find workarounds that negate effort-saving features; or you'll stop using the technology altogether. Automation must be easy to learn and easy to use.

Principle #3: Automation Must Improve Results

Reducing effort and ease of use aren't enough. Automation typically requires a significant investment of time and money, so there must be a larger, long-term payoff. The technology must also produce better results, such as increasing the flow of top talent and improved reporting to monitor the effectiveness of each hiring step. Only then is the technology worth incorporating into your process.

What happens when you implement automation that doesn't meet all three principles? Your hiring process slows or breaks down.

Automating references checks is a good example. The traditional methods of calling a candidate's references can be frustrating. First, you have to get the reference giver on the phone. That could take days of phone tag and follow up. When you get them on the phone, they may decline to answer your questions. Instead, they quote a company policy about being allowed only to confirm the job candidate's previous role and dates of employment.

CEOs from two organizations in the same Texas town were comparing notes on this reference checking challenge. One ran a large nonprofit, the other a mid-sized accounting consultancy. Both had made High Velocity Hiring part of their overall strategy.

The CEOs met regularly, sharing ideas and helping each other solve problems. One of their companies had recently found a solution for checking references—an online service. The service promised to save an hour of effort for each candidate. Plus, the service provider offered case studies showing how their approach improved the quality of hires. The CEOs decided to have their companies give it a try and compare their results.

Both companies ended up having similar experiences. Setting up each candidate in the service's online portal was simple. This took only a few minutes. The system then took it from there. Automated reference checking reduced effort. The results, though, were a different story. Each company had an uptick in failed hires after automating reference checking.

Does this mean automating reference checks doesn't work? No. It didn't work for these two companies. Both found that a conversation with a reference giver uncovered additional details and resulted in better hires.

Making Lean Recruiting your standard for choosing automation has a number of benefits. You'll cut through the myths, adopting only those technologies that enhance your Talent Accelerator Process. You'll make smarter choices that keep your TAP flowing.

How do you apply the three principles of Lean Recruiting? By reviewing important questions and running a test. You'll first answer questions about the need for a particular technology. If your answers validate the need, you'll conduct a test of the technology before making a commitment.

Here are the questions your hiring team should answer as you evaluate technology:

- Why do we need this automation?

- How will we use it?

- How will it reduce effort?

- Does it appear easy to implement? Learn? Use?

- What results must it achieve to be worth the time and money?

In answering the question, watch out for the myths. Are they driving the desire for automation? If so, address those myths immediately. Never let myths become the motive for choosing technology.

When it appears that automation is being considered for the correct motives, run a test. Ask the vendor for the opportunity to test-drive their product. During this experiment, measure the results. Does it reduce effort? How much? Have you found it easy to learn and use? Does it achieve the desired results? How do those results measure up when compared to how you get work done without that automation?

Only adopt automation that clearly meets all three principles of Lean Recruiting. No matter how exciting that automation may be. Walking away from something that seems cool can be hard. You're not alone when faced with this challenge. It's another aspect of human nature.

Avoiding the Extremes

Throughout the book, I've touched on human nature. Why? Regardless of who we are, where we live, and our line of work, our humanity is a common thread.

One aspect of human nature is seeking out the extremes. We tend to be all-in or completely out. If you've watched poker players, you've seen this dynamic in action. When players have a bad hand, they fold quickly. When they have a great hand (or are bluffing), they'll bet everything they have.

People also go to extremes with technology. Some are overly reliant on technology, while others avoid it as much as possible. Both extremes are harmful.

Organizations with an unhealthy reliance on automation suffer from technological codependency. They can't live without it. The technology runs the show. How work gets done is planned around its capabilities. When their tech can't do something, that obstacle becomes the reason it shouldn't be done. They go as far as using technology in ways it wasn't intended. Instead of technology serving the organization's people, the people become slaves to their technology.

One of the worst cases of technological codependency I've witnessed was at a biotech firm in Germany. The firm had it all when it came to hiring tech—a talent management system, multiple job boards, automated resume parsing, a candidate sourcing system, skills testing software. These were some of the products the firm was hooked on. But the hiring process was slow and ineffective.

The firm's various tech products weren't linked, requiring users to enter the same data several times. When leaders wanted specific hiring reports, they couldn't get them. The system didn't track that information. Searching the talent database was cumbersome, as was the skills-testing software. Hiring results suffered. Seats remained empty for months. Turnover was high: Two out of three new hires lasted less than a year.

On the opposite end of the spectrum, when organizations shun automation, they suffer from automation anorexia. Underutilization makes work harder. Tasks that could be handled in seconds by technology require hours of someone's valuable time. Work that could be done flawlessly through automated means is completed haphazardly. Automation anorexia makes hiring a long, frustrating process.

A law firm in the northwestern United States is a classic example of automation anorexia. The firm is as low-tech as it gets. They've avoided hiring technology completely. There's no ATS, no job boards, zero automation. Nothing.

The law firm runs newspaper ads when jobs become open. Resumes stream over their fax machine, flooding them with paper. Reviewing them takes hours. Frequently, none of these candidates are a fit, so they run another ad—another flood of resumes and hours of extra work. Once they find a good candidate, often it's too late. Another firm has already snapped them up.

Smartly, they keep the resumes of these good candidates. Their resumes fill four cabinets full of paper files. The firm searches these files every time they have an opening. Sifting through resumes takes hours and is always interrupted by competing demands. Much of the time the firm comes up empty-handed and has to run yet another ad. Filling a job ends up taking months.

How can you avoid the extremes of technological codependency and automation anorexia? Here are three ways:

1. **Use just enough:** The Talent Accelerator Process is already fast and accurate. Using enough of the right automation as part of your TAP helps keep talent flowing and hires happening quickly. How much is enough? This varies. Most organizations find they need at least an applicant tracking system and a job board that fits their version of TAP. The more hires you make using TAP, the greater your need may be for additional automation. Following the three principles of Lean Recruiting will guide you in using just enough technology for your circumstances.

2. **Keep the myths in check:** The myths can sneak up on you. New products may profess to be better than traditional hiring methods, when in reality they're not. It could appear that tech can cure process woes. Don't be deceived. The latest and greatest innovation may be what all the cool companies are buying. Make sure it's really what you need. Technology is neither the enemy nor the savior. It is but a tool. Picking appropriate automation that enhances your TAP requires keeping the myths constantly in check.

3. **Monitor your tech diet:** Staying lean requires a healthy diet. Too much tech creates a bloated process. Too little makes it weak. A healthy diet of just enough of the right tech will help you sustain a fast and accurate TAP.

Advice for Technology Vendors

Is your technology lean? Does it reduce effort while also being easy to use? Does it improve hiring results? You likely answered "yes." Most people do. Why wouldn't you? I'm sure you believe in what you offer and are proud of its capabilities.

If you are a tech vendor, I suggest taking time to honestly assess the leanness of your offerings, including asking users for their feedback. Every technology company that's taken time to do so has found something that could be leaner. In fact, the deeper they looked, the more opportunities they found to make their product compliant with the principles of Lean Recruiting.

Why does technology end up not being lean? Because the principles of Lean Recruiting are overlooked. This is unintentional. Most of the people I've met who create hiring technologies care about their customers and want to give them quality tools that improve their work. Unfortunately, many technology companies lack a process for ensuring that changes to their product always match all three principles.

You can see an example of the importance of process when you compare two popular applicant-tracking systems (ATSs).

Both products are good, made by companies full of smart people. As is common in software companies, both are innovating their products and striving to make them better. How each went about innovating their latest releases, however, was different.

The first ATS company looked at potential changes through the lens of Lean Recruiting. The development team carefully considered every idea. Each one had to pass a Lean Test, which started with three questions:

- Will the change reduce effort?

- Will it make things easier for users?

- Will it improve results?

(continued)

If the answer to all three was "yes," the company added that change to their list of features they planned to upgrade. If the answer to any was "no," that change was discarded, no matter how cool the idea seemed.

The Lean Test had one last step: Each change had to be examined in relationship to the overall software system. It would do no good to make one thing better, only to cause problems elsewhere. Improvements that passed this last step were deemed Lean Recruiting compliant and were added to the next software release.

The second ATS company brainstormed lots of possibilities for their upcoming release. Some of these ideas were requests from current customers. Others came from prospects who were interested in buying the software, but only if features were added. Pleasing current customers and winning new ones were important, so the company did everything it could to make these requests work. The development team was mindful about making the next version of the software as effortless as possible. They also prided themselves on keeping it easy to use. Balancing all of these factors was a challenge, but in the end they thought they'd built a better version of their product.

How'd each company do? Customers of the first company gave the new version of the software a thumbs-up. Common comments included: "It's faster than ever," "Many aspects are easier to use," and "I'm getting better results with this new release."

Customers of the second company gave the software mixed reviews. They liked some things, but not others. Comments included: "This takes too many steps," "This new feature is too difficult to use," and "I like this change, but its related tasks now take longer."

I know this sounds cold, but process is more important than people. No matter how smart those people may be. Smart people who follow a well-thought-out results-oriented process always have the end in mind. They don't

(continued)

get attached to ideas, focusing instead on outcomes. The process helps them keep ideas that work and let go of the rest. That's why the first of the two companies succeeded. They followed a process for baking Lean Recruiting into their new release. It's also why the second company failed. Their team of smart developers intended to make their release better. Unfortunately, they lacked a process to focus their efforts.

How can you make Lean Recruiting compliance part of your product development process? Here are three ways to begin:

1. **Focus on results, not ideas:** Technologists make a common mistake: They fall in love with their own ideas. They become so attached to them, they have trouble letting them go, even when they don't improve results. Maintaining a focus on results makes it easier to let go of features that don't make things better.

2. **Remember that a little becomes a lot:** Reducing effort isn't always about big things. Often, it's the little ones that matter just as much. Hiring has lots of repetitive tasks. When each repetition takes an extra minute, those minutes add up. As you reduce effort, pay attention to efforts big and small, striving to reduce each.

3. **Use the Lean Test:** Let the Lean Test guide your product updates, requests for new features, and the development of new technologies. Ask questions about every idea. Will the idea reduce effort? Is it easy to use? Will it improve users' results? Will it keep other aspects of your product lean? Retain the features that keep the product lean and discard the rest.

A final suggestion: Make Lean Recruiting a top goal. Why? It makes technology irresistible. Technology that reduces effort, is easy to use, and creates better results will sell itself.

Leaning Your TAP

Adding technology isn't the only way to keep your TAP lean. Over time, you'll find ways to creatively reduce effort, make aspects of your TAP easier to use, and improve your hiring results.

How can you keep leaning out your TAP? Five examples follow.

Example #1: Assigning Hire-Right Profiles

Employees who all do the same job can help write the Hire-Right Profiles for that role. These employees have different strengths. One of them may be really good at prioritizing. Another may be the best at performing detailed tasks. Someone else could be a savvy problem solver. Their different strengths are their areas of subject-matter expertise. When it comes to those aspects of the job, they know better than anyone, including you, what it takes to do quality work.

Have these employees collaborate to create a Hire-Right Profile for their role. In minutes, you can lay out the four-quadrant structure. Explain Dealmakers, Dealbreakers, Boosts, and Blocks by providing examples for each.

Assigning this to your team is an acknowledgment: You're demonstrating your trust in them. Let them handle the scheduling and logistics. If they want do this over lunch, offer to supply food. If they'd rather do it after hours, pay them for that time. By being flexible, you're showing your appreciation for this responsibility you've asked them to take on.

You can also have your staff handle Hire-Right Profile updates. They see what's going on with their coworkers. When new hires aren't working out, they know it before you do. If aspects of the day-to-day work are changing, they experience it first. Who better to update your profiles than the people living the job each day?

Assigning Hire-Right Profiles still takes effort. But that effort is concentrated, focused, and efficient.

Example #2: Crowdsourced Referrals

You've probably heard the expression that two's company and three's a crowd. When hiring, though, a crowd is powerful. Especially when you get their help with candidate referrals.

You have access to many different crowds: Employees that report to you, colleagues in other departments, peers in other companies, alums from college, family, and friends. These crowds are easily accessible through social media, email, and text.

The people in your crowds can help you with referrals. This doesn't mean you'll stop asking for them yourself. I'm suggesting that your crowds can help lighten the load. Asking for their help is one of the easiest forms of automation. People like being helpful.

Requesting help from your crowds can be quick and simple. You could send a text message to a group of people from time to time. Social media is perfect for a quick post about a specific type of candidate you're looking for.

Your appeals for help can also be creative. Gamifying your request (turning a task into a game) will quickly capture the interest of some of the crowd. For example, you could create a competitive game in a social media post. Your offer? The first three people to send a quality candidate referral could get to join you for drinks after work.

Crowds are a powerful force when you engage them as part of your hiring process. That force grows as you keep them engaged.

Example #3: Candidate-Driven Interviews

Interviewing isn't something that only happens during hiring. Lots of jobs—like being a journalist, an admissions counselor, or a researcher—require interviewing skills as an essential part of the daily work. When that's the case, one of the tools in your hiring toolkit should be the candidate-driven interview. This form of interview helps you evaluate the candidate as you watch them do the work they'd be hired to do.

How does the candidate-driven interview work? You bring two candidates into the room simultaneously, and they interview one another. You take notes as you watch them in action. There's a lot to observe. You'll experience how they interact, ask questions, manage the conversation, and relate to one another.

Candidate-driven interviews are a perfect example of streamlining your TAP. It's easy to set up and minimizes what you need to do. The results speak for themselves: You get to have a real experience of candidates doing important sample work.

Example #4: Responsive Reference Checks

To confirm that someone is a good hire, it's important to use reference checks. Chasing down reference givers, however, can be frustrating. Leaning your reference checking process can help.

It starts when a candidate passes your phone interview. Ask them to contact their reference givers the moment your conversation ends. Suggest that they ask each reference giver for options about when it's best to schedule reference calls.

Now you may be wondering: "Why would I want to take this step now? I mean, I don't know if I'm going to be offering this candidate a job yet." The reason: You do this because later on it'll eliminate phone tag and will speed up the process when you're ready to make a hire. Plus, you'll experience how your candidate takes direction and follows through. Their actions will also demonstrate their level of interest in your job.

Example #5: Delegated Check-Ins

To keep your Talent Inventory fresh, you'll want to periodically touch base with the people on your list. Touching base—using a lean approach—goes something like what is explained next.

I tell the prospective hire I want to remain in regular contact. Doing so allows me to keep them updated on when we might start working together. Also, it allows me to be a resource. I hear things all the time. Sometimes, that information can help others, like sharing details on a book I've recently read or an announcement I heard about a new seminar. Staying in touch lets me pass along helpful insights.

I go on to suggest that it's best if they call me, especially if they're currently working. I wouldn't want to catch them at a bad time. Maybe, I'd end up calling when the boss is standing in their office. They know when they can talk freely. I ask the candidate to check in monthly and to call me sooner if anything important changes in their work life.

Delegating check-ins ticks all the boxes for the principles of Lean Recruiting. It lessens effort and improves results. Staying in touch becomes meaningful to both you and your prospective employee. Also, it's another opportunity to experience their ability to follow through.

These five examples of leaning your TAP are just the beginning. You'll discover others ways to fine-tune your process. Keep watching and asking yourself how you can keep things easy, effective, and effortless.

Striking a Balance

In the season two opener of the TV series, *Mr. Robot*, a psychological thriller about a young computer hacker, a woman experiences technology gone wild. She lives in a fully automated apartment where technology controls everything. After arriving home one day, things go haywire. Lights brighten and dim as if they have free will. Her thermostat behaves erratically, turning her place into an icebox. The television turns itself on and blasts her with audio. Her burglar alarm sounds, and she's unable to turn it off. After a while, she's had enough and dashes out the door.[1]

Challenges with your hiring technologies probably won't make you want to run from your office. Nor will technology solve every problem. The right technology that fits your process will be an asset—a valuable, yet imperfect asset, made by smart and fallible people.

Striking a balance, when it comes to automation, is the best strategy. You can use too little or too much automation. Use just enough technology that fits your Talent Accelerator Process, and you'll constantly be able to hire in an instant.

Action List for Chapter 9

I'm sure technology has improved your work and life. If your experience with tech is like mine, you've also had frustrations. You've made choices you've later regretted, buying products that failed to do what you expected. To avoid these regrets with hiring technologies, take the steps that follow.

Be a Mythbuster

Watch out for the technology myths. They could be affecting your decisions now, and can surface at any time. Technology is constantly growing and changing. The allure of automation makes it incredibly attractive, even seductive. Be certain that you're picking hiring technologies for the correct reasons.

Find and Eliminate Bloat

Your hiring process could already be bloated with technology that has fattened it up with unnecessary effort. As you implement the Talent Accelerator Process, assess your current technologies. Do they fit your faster process? Do they match the three principles of Lean Recruiting? Use the questions earlier in this chapter to determine which of your current technologies you'll keep and which you'll replace.

Make the Lean Recruiting Principles Your Standard

By implementing the Talent Accelerator Process, you're taking a stand. You're committing to a hiring process that's streamlined. Making the Lean Recruiting principles an organizational standard will strengthen that commitment.

Lean Recruiting is like an insurance policy. It protects you from loss—losing time and money on automation that doesn't fit your faster way of hiring.

The importance of Lean Recruiting has prompted some organizations to create groups responsible for its enforcement. Called Lean Recruiting watch groups, they're charged with ensuring the principles are consistently maintained.

Encourage Your Vendors

Technology vendors are valuable partners. Partnerships thrive on communication, including what's working and what's not.

The best partners encourage one another, helping each other be successful.

Ask your technology vendors to make Lean Recruiting compliance their standard. Show them where their products aren't easy to use. Provide feedback on features that need to be made effortless. Ask for the results you need for your Talent Accelerator Process. If your vendor can't meet your needs for leaner technology, move on to a vendor who can.

Keep Leaning Out Your TAP

Give the five examples for leaning your TAP a try. Invent your own, too. Organizations around the globe have found hundreds of ways to fine-tune their TAP. Start by experimenting with ways of reducing effort that also improve results.

CHAPTER
10

Engage Talent Scouts

Create Lasting Partnerships
Between Organizations
and Staffing Providers

Effective recruiting and hiring in the world of business is a lot like fielding a team in Major League Baseball (MLB). According to the baseball rulebook, on any given day, each major league team in North America can suit up 25 players. But that doesn't mean each team has only 25 players to choose from. In fact, they have more. Many more.

Every major league team has an "expanded roster" with fifteen additional players who are immediately available if needed. Also, each team has a "farm system" of seven to 10 minor league teams. This gives them another 150 to 200 or more players to call on. Teams can trade players with other teams. They also employ talent scouts. These scouts work in countries across the globe, funneling additional talent to both the major and minor league clubs.

This coordinated approach is why MLB teams always have someone to fill every role, the instant they're needed. A game is never cancelled because there aren't enough players. Nor is a position ever left open. There are always nine players in the starting lineup. Leaders in baseball know that it's not a matter of "if" they will need additional talent, but "when." So, they plan for the when.

The roster of employees at your company is ever changing. People leave; jobs are created; promotions happen; new business comes in. All of which generates open seats. Just like baseball, it is never a matter of if a job will open, but when.

Large organizations, and some mid-market companies, have their own talent scouts (a talent acquisition department or corporate recruiters). Small companies with HR staff make scouting talent part of their job. However, these in-house employees aren't always able to source enough people to fill all of the open jobs. That's why organizations of all sizes also rely on an external scouting arm—employment services often referred to as staffing companies or recruitment firms. They are part of a global staffing industry supplying temporary employees and candidates for full-time employment.

The staffing industry has grown from a handful of temp agencies started after World War II,[1] to 20,000 staffing companies in the United States alone.[2] Globally, the industry helps 60 million people a year in their job life.[3] The positive impact of external talents scouts is why they're one of the eight talent streams of candidate gravity.

One of the things that make this talent stream unique is that it comes with a guarantee. External talent scouts frequently guarantee their "product." If a temporary worker you bring in has poor attendance, the staffing agency will typically provide a replacement person. When the contract employee you secure for a project doesn't work out, the firm representing that employee will send someone else. Full-time hires also come with guarantees, such as a replacement candidate or a refund of the fee paid for the recruiting services.

The guarantee provided by external talent scouts adds a level of safety in using their services. This guarantee is valuable—hiring on your own comes with no such promises. There's also the flexibility gained when using temporary workers. Temp workers allow your company to scale your workforce as business ebbs and flows. Also, engaging an external talent scout is "free" in most instances. Your company pays a placement fee for a full-time hire or an hourly rate for a temporary worker only if the scout delivers the person you need. Given just these three benefits, it would be reasonable to expect that many companies rely on external talent scouts. They don't. Less than a third of organizations use their services each year.[4]

Why aren't more organizations using external talent scouts? It isn't that companies aren't hiring. With the exception of the smallest of companies, I've found that almost all organizations need talent every year (and often many times throughout the year). Nor is it that do-it-yourself hiring is making the need for outside help unnecessary. In 2016, 40 percent of employers reported difficulty with filling jobs.[5]

I've asked thousands of organizations that aren't regular users of staffing or recruitment firms: "Why don't you use them (or use them more often)?" For 30 years, I've heard the same answers:

- "They often don't have the talent I need when I need it."

- "They're expensive."

- "I've had a bad experience."

- "Outside agencies are a necessary evil."

The complaints don't stop there. External talent scouts voice their share of frustrations about working with organizations. They say things like:

- "They treat us like a commodity and pressure us to lower our price."

- "We submit candidates for their consideration, but hear nothing back."

- "HR sees us as competition."

Not all relationships between organizations and external scouts are contentious. Many organizations appreciate their staffing providers, and lots of external scouts have positive experiences with the organizations they serve. But there's also a growing group of organizations and scouts that have formed even better relationships—relationships that have eliminated complaints on both sides.

How have they done this? They've formed partnerships based upon mutuality: A belief that, for the relationship to succeed, each party must get its needs met. The organization gets the talent it needs when it's needed. The talent scout is equitably compensated for the value it provides. Both meet expectations that make the partnership work.

Such partnerships achieve a greater good by creating better outcomes for job candidates. Like a nurturing home resulting from a healthy marriage, these partnerships foster positive work environments. Workers benefit from the healthy dynamics of the relationship. I've heard workers refer to these partnerships as heroic. That's why these business relationships are referred to as heroic partnerships.

This chapter will help you form these heroic partnerships. The pages that follow are meant to be read by both organizations and staffing providers. You'll learn about the different ways partners work together. I'll share examples of what happens when you create mutually beneficial relationships. You'll also learn about the five expectations that form the foundation of how you'll work together.

An Ecosystem of Services

The staffing industry has evolved into an ecosystem of workforce solutions—an ecosystem that continues to grow and change (Figure 10.1). Weighing your options can be overwhelming.

You could choose a search firm to hire a full-time employee. Their recruiters will conduct a search for qualified candidates matching your specifications. You'll get to interview these candidates. Find one that fits the job? You can hire that individual and pay a placement fee to the firm for their services.

Then, there's temporary staffing (also referred to as contract staffing for IT, creative, engineering, and other professional roles). Temporary staffing allows you to bring in one, a handful, or hundreds of workers for a specified period of time. The workers are employed by the staffing firm; you are typically responsible for supervising their work. When there is a large number of workers, the firm supplying them may also provide an on-site coordinator. You'll pay the staffing firm for each hour someone works. The contract you sign may have provisions for converting temporary workers to full-time employees of your company

FIGURE 10.1	The Workforce Solutions Ecosystem

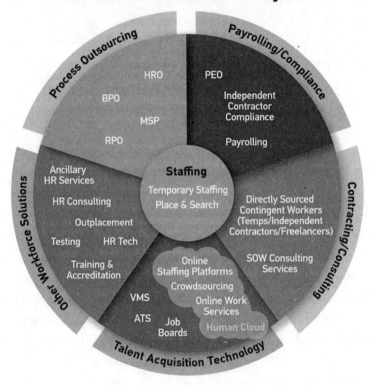

Staffing Industry Analysts'
Workforce Solutions Ecosystem

www.staffingindustry.com | ©2016 Crain Communications Inc

(called temp-to-hire). Some temporary staffing firms also provide place and search services for full-time employees.

Need more options? An alphabet soup of valuable offerings is available:

- **BPO—Business Process Outsourcing:** An entire work function or department, such as your mailroom or call center, is handled by an outside organization.

- **HRO—Human Resource Outsourcing:** Your provider takes over portions of your human resource function.

- **MSP—Managed Service Provider:** An outside vendor manages the staffing firms supplying your company with workers.

- **RPO—Recruitment Process Outsourcing:** You transfer all or part of your recruitment process to an external service provider.

- **SOW—Statement of Work:** An outside vendor becomes responsible for a defined set of work activities and deliverables.

- **VMS—Vendor Management System:** An Internet-based solution helps you manage and procure staffing services.

Need even more possibilities? How about a freelancer who's part of the gig economy? Online platforms are allowing an increasing number of people to go it on their own. These platforms create a "human cloud" of workers ready for hire. You'll likely never meet them in person because tasks and payments are all managed online.

If you're convinced, after reading this list of possibilities, that you know exactly which solution is best for you, be careful. Picking a solution because it sounds like it fits is no better than self-prescribing medication. A TV ad about a new drug may convince us we need it. Better to let an expert, our doctor, help us make an informed choice. The same is true when choosing a workforce solution. It's best to let the experts lay out the best options for your circumstances.

What happens when organizations self-prescribe a workforce solution? Sometimes it works out; other times it does not. There's the bank that was convinced that VMS was the way to go. It slowed down their hiring. An MSP proved to be a better solution. Then there's the insurance company that set its sights on RPO. It failed. SOW consulting services was what they really needed for their call center. There's also the publishing company that fell in love with BPO. What an expensive mistake that turned out to be. Using temporary staffing worked out much better.

Heroic partnerships begin by picking a good partner, not by fixating on a solution. A good partner will take time to understand your organization and its needs. Then, they'll walk you through your options. The right staffing partner (the name I'll use from here on to refer to the companies that provide the various workforce solutions) can do more than help keep jobs filled. They can become an indispensable part of your business.

Extreme Loyalty

Ask anyone in the staffing industry, and they'll tell you that clients come and go. You'll occasionally hear stories of long-term relationships that span years. But not every staffing firm can say they've retained dozens of the most prominent U.S. companies as loyal customers for years. Some, for over a decade. Staff Management | SMX, headquartered in Illinois, has achieved this. One of their relationships has lasted 28 years.

Staff Management | SMX is part of TrueBlue, the largest industrial staffing firm in the United States. It seems fitting that they fall under the TrueBlue umbrella. The definition of the phrase "true blue" is to be extremely loyal. The long-term customers of Staff Management | SMX fit this definition. "Our six brands serve 130,000 organizations each year, providing them with over 800,000 workers," said Patrick Beharelle, TrueBlue's president and chief operating officer. "Every one of our brands has maintained long-term relationships with thousands of companies. Staff Management | SMX has an exceptional base of loyal customers."

Why do customers stick with Staff Management | SMX? Let's look at that manufacturer that's been working with them for 28 years. Mary, their procurement manager, says it's because of the quality of the relationship. "We don't mandate that our manufacturing sites work with Staff Management | SMX. However, over 90 percent do. Staff Management | SMX has proven themselves by doing quality work at site after site. Winning our trust has allowed them to expand organically through internal recommendations."

Mary made clear how important staffing is to her organization when she said, "Failure is not an option. Our company is dependent on our temp labor program to meet our production requirements. The on-site managed model we use allows Staff Management | SMX to be a seamless part of our organization. Beyond filling our staffing requirements, they understand our culture and find candidates that are truly a 'good fit.'"

Mary's been with the manufacturer for a few years. I asked her to compare the partnership with Staff Management | SMX to her previous experiences. "The nature of the long-term relationship we have with Staff Management | SMX is different from what I've seen in other organizations," she said. "At my last employer, there was a hard-and-fast rule to drive competition and reduce costs. Relationships with vendors were nonexistent—there was a transactional attitude toward the purchase."

This transactional approach created other issues: "There was no big picture, since procurement of staffing wasn't looked at from a strategic perspective. It was all about dollars and cents. If we wanted something better, cheaper, or different, we'd wait to see what was offered during the next RFP period. Once a desired solution was identified, we were told to have the vendors 'sharpen their pencils' when it came to pricing. This usually led to a race to the bottom with vendors reducing their offerings to the bare bones to win the bid. In the end no one was truly satisfied. With Staff Management | SMX it's different."

How does Staff Management | SMX do it? "We're looking for partners . . . organizations where we can integrate our solutions and become part of their company," said Loree Lynch, Vice President of Operations for Staff Management | SMX. She's been around for all 28 years of their partnership with the manufacturer. "Our job is to look out for their business. We do everything we can to protect their brand, not just look out for our own brand."

Identifying good partners starts with their sales process. "We're not a good fit for every organization," said Lynch. "Nor is every company a good fit for us. We improve how our customers get work done and are compensated for that impact. If a prospect is looking to put bodies in jobs, or is purely driven by price, we go our separate ways."

The partnership approach at Staff Management | SMX continues through every step. "We bring in an engagement team early on in the sales process," said Lynch. "It includes people from sales and operations who conduct a needs assessment." The engagement team remains intact through each stage of the partnership. They design flexible solutions, present them to the customer, and drive implementation. "Our approach is methodical. We kick off implementation by getting all of the client stakeholders in the room. We discuss expectations—theirs and ours. We get everything on the table so we all have a clear understanding of what is expected and by whom. It lays the groundwork for a lasting partnership."

And last these partnerships do. The on-site services teams at Staff Management | SMX client sites become entrenched in the customers' business. They sit in on production meetings and become part of their safety committees. Frequently, it's hard to figure out who works for Staff Management | SMX and who's an employee of the customer. What's easy to figure out is the impact. Customers say their expectations have been met or exceeded, rating Staff Management | SMX in the top 2 percent of staffing agencies in the United States.

More Than Just a Matchmaker

Are heroic partnerships the exclusive domain of big staffing partners that provide large-scale services? No. Small and mid-sized firms are forming them as well. Size of firm and scale of service don't matter. What does is building mutually beneficial relationships.

UK-based Serocor Group isn't a big, publicly traded company like TrueBlue. But its business units have made a big difference for their customers. Each unit zeroes in on a different set of needs. One specializes in engineering and IT. Another targets the digital space. Yet another division helps organizations in the cyber, defense, and security markets. Plus, Serocor has developed its own Recruitment Process Outsourcing service.

Specialization is one way Serocor's divisions have developed lasting partnerships with customers. "Many of our competitors focus on delivering people," said Mike Gawthorne, Serocor's CEO. "We deliver expertise, using that knowledge to help our customers build better organizations." Gawthorne has grown the company with this idea in mind. "We've built a team of recruiters who are subject matter experts. They have vast knowledge of the industries they serve."

Gawthorne's strategy for sharing expertise is straightforward: They unselfishly give it away. Even to companies that aren't paying customers. "Our recruiters are a combination thought leader and matchmaker. Their job is to constantly deliver value to everyone they're in contact with. This starts with prospective customers. We share market intelligence and best practices. If a company elects not to work with us, they're still better off from having interacted with our team. For those that become customers, we use our expertise to shape the solutions we deliver to them."

Has this paid off? It has. Most of Serocor's customers make them their exclusive recruiting partner. This level of trust in a single firm is uncommon. Many companies hedge their bets, pitting several firms against one another.

To continue their success, Gawthorne focuses on expectations. "Expectations are the key to success in the recruitment business. This starts with high expectations for our team. Every member of our team must operate with integrity and deliver value to every relationship. We expect our candidates to communicate honestly and do their best work. Our relationships with every customer are founded on clear expectations. We know what they expect. They know what we expect. That's why so many of our relationships are exclusive. We trust each other."

Clear and Reasonable Expectations

What do all heroic partnerships have in common? Expectations. Organizations and staffing partners who've formed heroic partnerships have communicated their expectations to one another.

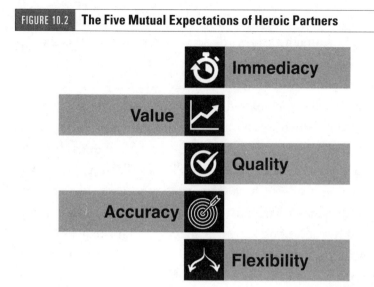

| FIGURE 10.2 | The Five Mutual Expectations of Heroic Partners |

These expectations are clear and reasonable, and are centered upon making their relationship mutually beneficial.

Five mutual expectations form the foundation of heroic partnerships. Each expectation creates a layer of stability. The more of these layers that are in place, the stronger the foundation, and the greater the likelihood the relationship will stand the test of time.

What are these clear and reasonable expectations? They fall into five categories (Figure 10.2).

Expectation #1: Flexibility

If you work for an organization, you must be flexible. It's important to remember there are no "purple squirrels"—absolutely perfect candidates with every skill and experience imaginable. These candidates don't exist. Your staffing partners, then, can't manufacture talent from scratch. Providing realistic Hire-Right Profiles to your staffing partner will help them do great work for you.

If you're a staffing partner, you too must remain flexible. The needs of the organizations you serve are changing constantly. A sudden influx of orders can be followed by a lull. New regulations can create an immediate need for candidates with a different skillset. Projects pop up and initiatives slow down.

It's your job to understand the shifting needs in each relationship. Does the company have a busy season? A slow period? How is their industry changing? In what ways will this change affect their hiring needs? Who are their competitors? How do these competitors impact the business of your customer? You need to keep asking questions, so you're always ready to be helpful.

Flexibility is expectation #1 for a reason. Without it, your partnership may get off the ground, but it won't last long.

Expectation #2: Accuracy

If you're a leader in an organization, you have vital information. You know your organization's goals and the work that needs to be done to reach them. You're the one who sees what's going on, including how things are changing. Sometimes, those changes impact the type of help you need. It's your job to communicate these details. If you do, you're enabling your partner's success. If you don't, you're setting them up for failure.

If you're a staffing partner, you're a matchmaker. This begins with the details. Do you have all the details you need to match your customer with the right solution? Have you done this type of work for the customer in the past? If so, have you explored how the work may be different this time, or assumed everything is the same? Matchmaking should never begin until you know you've got all of the current details.

Regardless of your delivery mechanism—temporary staffing, search, RPO, BPO, SOW—it's your responsibility to match customers with the appropriate solution. Does this mean you'll always be the one to deliver that solution? No, heroic partners are honest about their limitations. They willingly refer business to companies better suited to meet a customer's needs.

In a heroic partnership, accuracy fortifies your foundation, keeping your relationship rock solid.

Expectation #3: Quality

As a staffing partner, the organizations you work with demand quality. But what comprises quality? One aspect is in delivering the most qualified people. Another aspect is the caliber of your service. The competency of your staff also comes into play, as does the quality of ongoing customer support. Quality is multifaceted.

How do you ensure you're always delivering quality? Never guess. Ask your customer how they define quality, and tell them how you'll deliver that quality. Then keep your promises. Be sure to back up those promises with competent people who provide excellent support.

Your organization's staffing partners also require quality— quality feedback during each stage of the process. They need your honest feedback on service proposals, helpful comments about resumes they've sent for review, detailed comments after interviews, and regular input during ongoing projects. Without this feedback, they're flying blind. Your input will directly impact the quality of their work.

A mutual focus on quality anchors your heroic partnership, ensuring it remains on solid ground.

Expectation #4: Value

Even the best partnerships can fail around monetary expectations. If your organization expects lots of value for little money, it will undermine your staffing partner. Without healthy margins, they won't be able to sustain quality work. To keep their business viable, they'd have to "cheat" on you, skimping on services and sending top talent to better-paying customers. Eventually, the relationship will break down.

Does this mean your organization should pay inflated prices? Of course not. Your organization should pay for value. The greater the value, the more you must be willing to invest. The value you receive isn't just the services themselves. It includes how your partner improves your organization's productivity, efficiency, and profitability. Your staffing partners deserve equitable compensation for the value they provide.

As a staffing partner, you can't engage in pricing extremes. Charge too much and you'll erode your partner's trust. Charge too little and you're jeopardizing your ability to do quality work. Your pricing must be directly proportionate to the value you deliver.

You must also give the organization options. There is no one-size-fits-all staffing solution. When your customers buy things, they're used to having choices. So it's only fitting you provide them with choices, too. Like any business that provides tiered options—a basic service, a deluxe service, and a premium service—you can create these types of choices for your buyers.

Heroic partners know that skimping will cause the foundation of their relationship to crack. That's why they keep their focus on value, not price.

Expectation #5: Immediacy

No one likes to wait. Delays will damage your partnership.

As a staffing partner, it's never a good idea to make customers wait. They need help now, not days from now. If you don't have what they need, when they need it, they'll reach out to someone else. Don't believe this is the case? Think about how you've won new business. You were at the right place at the right time with the right solution. If you're not capable of giving your partner what they need, there's someone else who can.

One of your service standards must be immediacy. Earlier in the book, I walked you through the seven principles of an on-demand system, and explained how these are incorporated into the Talent Accelerator Process. Make this part of your business strategy. Maintain an inventory of the core talent your customer will need. You'll be able to supply that talent on-demand, freeing you up to work on any additional needs they have as well.

Your organization must also act quickly if you expect your staffing partner to deliver positive results. Your input guides their work, helping them do quality work for you. Return their calls and emails swiftly. Provide prompt feedback on proposals, resumes, and interviews. Make nimble choices when choosing a solution or a person to hire. Immediacy also benefits your organization. The top talent provided by your partner will be sought out by your competitors. Taking immediate action makes sure these talented people end up working for you.

Adding in this final expectation makes the foundation of your partnership nearly impregnable. Immediacy makes it a relationship built to last.

Might there be other expectations you'll need to set? Yes. The five mutual expectations put your relationship on solid footing. As your partnership evolves, so too may your expectations. Making them clear and reasonable will keep your relationship solid, increasing the chances it serves both of your needs for a long time.

Choosing Your Partner

Setting mutual expectations is easiest when you pick the right partner. You'll have lots of potential partners to mull over. Organizations can select from an array of staffing industry vendors, and these vendors get to pick whom they do business with. Both of you should choose wisely since your relationship will impact workers' lives.

Staffing providers work with multiple customers. Organizations may also opt to work with more than one staffing partner. Barry Asin, president of research firm Staffing Industry Analysts, believes it's prudent to build relationships with at least several providers. "It's tough to expect one staffing company to do everything for you with equal skill," said Asin. "Relying on multiple firms can be a smart choice. Deciding on how many and which ones depends on several factors. These include how often you hire and the types of skills you seek. I'm continually intrigued at the increased level of specialization within the staffing industry and how resourceful staffing firms can be at finding specific types of workers."

Whether you decide to work with one or several staffing partners, how to find those that are the best fit for your organization is shared in the following sections.

Look Beyond Capabilities

When you review the website of a potential staffing partner, you'll probably find a list of their capabilities. Capabilities are great, but only if they produce the kind of outcomes you need. Dig deeper, looking for the results these capabilities have created for other organizations. Ask your potential partner for specifics. Whom have they served? What results did they achieve? How'd they achieve them? Expectations only work if your partner is able to meet them. Your upfront work in picking a capable partner who can meet your needs will pay off in the long run.

Check Out Their Known Associates

Is your prospective partner part of a reputable association? Does that association require its members to abide by

(continued)

a code of standards? Having worked with thousands of companies that provide workforce solutions, I've noticed an important pattern: Those that do the best work are part of a reputable association. As association members, they have access to timely information, legal updates, and ongoing education.

For instance, the American Staffing Association (ASA) offers myriad resources, white papers, and educational offerings to its members and their clients to ensure they remain up-to-date on critical employment and staffing-related laws and regulations. "Navigating through the increasingly complex array of federal, state, and local laws and court rulings designed to protect the rights and interests of the 16 million temporary and contract employees who worked for our industry in the past year is a daunting challenge," said Richard Wahlquist, ASA president and chief executive officer. "We are committed to keeping member companies informed of and compliant with all of the latest staffing laws and regulations so they can be valued business partners with their clients." ASA also offers four professional certification programs for staffing professionals, all of which concentrate on applicable labor and employment and labor law knowledge.

You'll find a list of associations in the Appendix to help you get started in finding a partner.

Sweat the Small Stuff

Small details make a big difference. Pay attention to the little things as you get to know your potential partner. Do you have to repeat details they missed the first time you shared them? Does it take them minutes or days to return calls and emails? Do they follow through on commitments, such as sending a proposal or resume when promised? Selling is a courtship. Your potential partner is on their best behavior while they're trying to win you over. Their behaviors aren't likely to improve after you've committed to work with them. Consider if their "best behaviors" are what you want in a business relationship.

(continued)

If you're a staffing industry vendor, there are pointers to help you identify organizations that could be good partners.

Assess Alignment

Is your prospective customer's line of business a fit for you? Are the solutions or people they seek in your wheelhouse? What about their culture and ideals? How do those align with your own? These questions are straightforward but sometimes overlooked. Why? Salespeople. Some salespeople have yet to meet a client they didn't like, and they want to do business with everyone. These salespeople usually have the best intentions, as they want to serve others and bring business to their company. Unfortunately, their desire to help blinds them to the potential mismatch. It's difficult to agree on mutual expectations when you and your prospect aren't on the same page.

Check the Closet for Skeletons

Best to know up front if there are skeletons in your prospective partner's closet. Does their workplace have a bad reputation? Are they the subject of a regulatory, discriminatory, or criminal investigation? How about customer reviews online and employee chatter on Glassdoor.com? Are there patterns to what people say? What's in the press? How could bad news impact the work you'll do? Finding negative information about your prospect doesn't mean you should avoid doing business with them. Your service may be exactly what's needed for them to resolve an issue. It's prudent to know what you may be getting into. Being shocked by hidden skeletons should only happen in a haunted house.

See if They're Stuck

Many organizations engage in the old way of hiring. They're stuck in a slow process with lots of steps and many interviews. Is this the case with your potential partner? If so, be mindful. Your services can help them speed things up, but only if they're willing to change. Ask questions to gauge their interest in hiring faster. Share with them the new way of hiring, and how your solution has helped others speed things up. It's better to know now if your prospect is open to change or if they'll demand that you join them in the slow lane of hiring.

Collective Effort

As a parent, I know that the statement "It takes a village to raise a child" is true. My kids were influenced by a village as they grew up—family, friends, neighbors, teachers, coaches. My son and daughter are now adults, and who they are is a result of the people that surrounded them.

Filling jobs in an instant, and keeping them filled, also takes a village—a village with an organization that wants to keep jobs filled, staffing partners who can lend a hand, and hiring technology vendors who support them with lean automation. Their collective efforts help each other be successful. The organization has enough people to get work done. Staffing partners and technology vendors have sustainable businesses. The village also includes workers who go to positive work environments each day. All because of the heroic partnership.

Action List for Chapter 10

What follows is a summary of actions for organizations.

Take Another Look

Are you working with a staffing partner a little? Not at all? I suggest taking another look at how the staffing industry could help you hire faster and keep jobs filled.

Consider the reasons why your organization has low or no usage of staffing partners. Jot down all the reasons. Then look for patterns. Often, these reasons can be distilled into two or three issues. Use this short list of issues as you review possible partners. Look for a firm with a track record in solving these problems.

Review the Workforce Solutions Ecosystem Cautiously

It's good to know your options but not to become overly attached to any of them. Awareness of your options will help you have open-minded conversations with potential staffing partners. Stay alert to all the possibilities, including how several solutions could be combined for your unique circumstances.

Determine How Well You've Met the Five Expectations

Have you been flexible about available skillsets? Do you consistently provide your staffing partner with accurate updates? Are you giving them quality feedback? Do you focus on value instead of price? Are you responding swiftly? Would your partner agree with your answers? Meeting mutual expectations starts with cleaning up your side of the street.

Evaluate Your Current Staffing Partners

Review your current staffing partner(s). Have one with whom things aren't going well? Before moving on to a different vendor, it's worth exploring the five mutual expectations with them. Good partnerships don't always start off that way. You and your partner can learn from previous mistakes, using mutual expectations to create a heroic partnership.

When it's time to move on, it's a good idea to figure out what happened. Did you miss something when choosing the firm? Use the pointers for choosing partners listed in this chapter as a guide, so history doesn't repeat itself.

Next is a summary of actions for staffing partners.

List Your Complaints

What frustrates you about customers? What frustrates your coworkers? Get everyone in a room and make a list. Let it all out; vent if you need to. Take that list and organize the issues into categories, such as "being pressured about price" and "poor customer follow-through." These are the things you'll want to pay special attention to as you develop mutual expectations with existing and new customers.

Find Your Place in the Workforce Solutions Ecosystem

Should your firm offer other services in the Workforce Solutions Ecosystem? Maybe. Maybe not. Adding additional offerings must be done for the correct reason, not because your competitors are offering those services.

What's the correct reason? It's one that fits your endgame. Consider why you're in business. What you're trying to achieve for yourself and your customers. Let that guide what else, if anything, you add to your capabilities.

Staffing Industry Analysts, the creator of the Workforce Solutions Ecosystem graphic, has developed a detailed report you may find helpful. You can download it at www2.staffingindustry.com/Research/Free-Resources.

Determine How Well You've Done Your Part

Do you provide the flexibility your customers need? Are you a good matchmaker of solutions for their problems? Is quality inherent in everything you do and all that you provide? Do you offer scalable value and pricing, packaged into distinct options? Can your customers count on you to have what they need, when they need it? If we asked your customers these questions, how would their answers compare? Making these expectations your way of doing business will make your firm effective and attractive.

Include Talent Inventories as Part of Your Business Model

When do organizations need talent? Now, not days from now. Maintaining a Talent Inventory allows you to meet their needs immediately.

How's this work? Use the Talent Accelerator Process to develop an on-demand delivery system. The core roles in your inventory are the ones your customers need most.

Adopt Zero-to-Fill as Your Internal Standard

Go to almost any staffing or recruitment conference, and you'll hear people talk about their hiring challenges. They can't find enough recruiters, salespeople, or support staff. Some are perpetually understaffed and have been so for years. Every empty seat undermines serving customers, resulting in lost opportunities and profits. Why does this happen? These firms are so busy filling jobs for customers, they're not spending enough time keeping their own seats filled.

Treat your firm like it's your best customer. Make zero-to-fill your standard. Use the Talent Accelerator Process to fill your own jobs in an instant.

Durable Diversity

Maintain a Dependable Workforce of Complementary People

Is diversity important? Most organizational leaders answer with an immediate "yes." Why do they believe this? Those answers vary. Some say diversity has improved their business results. Others mention that it allows them to better serve their diverse customer base. Still others state diversity in hiring is the right thing to do in our modern world.

Diversity has been part of my life since childhood. I was fortunate to attend public schools and a state university filled with a diverse body of students and teachers. Classes and teams and student groups had a mixture of people. Some were quite smart and talented, others modestly so. Neither had anything to do with race, religion, gender, sexual orientation, or other dimensions of diversity. The achievements of my peers were based upon their efforts, not their backgrounds.

Let's be clear: I wasn't oblivious to prejudice as a kid and young adult. My friends shared their experiences about being "different." They talked about being stared at suspiciously, receiving extra scrutiny from police, and family members being passed over for jobs. All because they looked or acted differently. These stories angered me then, and still do today.

That's one of the reasons I was attracted to my first recruiting job. I've always believed that the most qualified person should get the job, regardless of their background. Which is why I was thrilled to serve on my first search committee in the late 1980s.

We were helping a college select a new director for their Career Planning and Placement office. In extending the invitation, the school stressed the importance of diversity. They'd reached out to a diverse pool of candidates. Administrators had whittled the list of contenders down to a handful of potential hires. Members of the search committee were to help make the final selection. This included a commitment that we'd choose the person who was the best fit for the role. I was excited. We were hiring for a department that helped other people find work. It seemed like a perfect match for my passion for supporting people in their careers.

To kick off our work, our committee met for a planning session. Leading the meeting was a vice president from the school. He thanked us for taking part and brought us up to speed on the status of the search. The college had reviewed fifty applicants for the director role. These applicants came from all parts of the country and were "a melting pot of diversity." He and his colleagues had identified the four best candidates. Our job was to interview them one at a time, compare notes, and rank them in order of whom we thought should be first choice, second choice, and so forth. The process sounded reasonable.

The vice president ended the meeting with the following charge: "Just so you know, one of our final four is a minority candidate. If he's qualified, rank him first. Any questions?" My first thought was: Did I hear that correctly? Did he tell us that being a minority was the most important of the criteria? I must have misunderstood. I raised my hand, and asked, "What if one of the other candidates is more qualified?" Narrowing his eyes, he glared at me. Then, he looked around the room, and responded, "Like I said, one of our final four is a minority candidate. If he's qualified, he's the one you should rank first. Any *other* questions?" There were none. The meeting was adjourned. Committee members grabbed their things and left the room quickly.

I was angry and embarrassed. Here I thought I would be taking part in something good. Something meaningful. Instead, I learned that the deck was already stacked in a way that seemed unfair. Plus, I was embarrassed by the vice president's stern response to my question. Most of all, I was shocked at the contradiction. The college had stressed the importance of diversity and had required that we commit to picking the best person for the job, regardless of their background.

I was tempted to quit. After a long mental debate, I stuck with the job. I can't say exactly why. It felt like something I had to do. I'm glad I did. We interviewed all four candidates, sharing our thoughts after each. Following the interviews, we did as we were asked: We ranked the candidates as our first choice, second choice, then third and fourth. Who'd we rank first? The minority candidate. Not because we were told to, but because he was the best person for the job.

No big deal, right? It all worked out in the end. Not exactly. The minority candidate accepted the job. Later, he learned what we'd been told—that he would have gotten the job if he were qualified, even if one of the other candidates was better qualified. He was appalled, nearly resigning his new post.

In the end, he stayed. He decided to use the circumstances of his hire and his director role to promote change. This included meeting one-on-one with each member of the search committee. It was a meeting I'll never forget.

The director asked me about my experience serving on the search committee. I was honest, telling him everything—my passion for recruiting, the mixed messages from the college and vice president, and my anger over what seemed like an unfair process. He responded, "That's good. I like that you're angry. It's appropriate to be angry about prejudicial hiring. Because that's what this was. Prejudice in action. Race, gender, or other factors should never trump fitness for a job. That's the problem with many diversity initiatives. People are put in jobs because they're a minority, not because they're the best fit. Some of them are put in roles for which they're ill prepared. Their careers and the organizations where they work end up being hurt."

At the end of our conversation, the director asked for a promise: "Promise me that you'll do what you can to promote a fair and sustainable form of diversity." It was a commitment I was happy to make.

Durable Diversity

Research backs up assertions that diversity has positive impacts. Companies with the most diverse workforces are more likely to generate better financial results.[1] In the United States, there's a direct relationship between financial performance and the amount of ethnic and racial diversity of the executive team.[2] The more women on an executive team, the better the company's results as well. Having 30 percent female executives generates up to six percentage points in additional profits.[3]

Does this mean that everyone is sold on the importance of a diverse workforce? No, they're not. When asked if diversity matters in the workplace, some leaders answer "no" or "I'm not sure." But not immediately. Initially, they'll look around, making sure no one else is listening, even shutting their doors. Sometimes, they've demanded a pledge of anonymity. Why the caution? They're afraid. They believe it's politically incorrect, when it comes to diversity in the workplace, to offer anything but an affirmative response.

Are these leaders bigots? A handful are, but not all. The majority of those who've shared doubts with me about diversity want to hire people with diverse backgrounds. They also want their jobs filled and to remain filled. For them, individual differences don't matter. What does is having enough qualified people to get work done.

For these leaders, diversity isn't the problem. The issue is how their organizations go about maintaining a diverse workforce. Like the aforementioned director of Career Planning and Placement, these leaders don't believe that skills and experience should take a back seat to diversity. They bristle when told to hire someone solely because of race. They take issue with meeting gender balance quotas. Religion, ethnicity, and sexual orientation, in their eyes, shouldn't be factors used in the selection process.

Adding to their frustration is the use of selection methods, like blind hiring, as a way to improve diversity. Blind hiring techniques include masking names on resumes and conducting anonymous interviews using chat rooms and voice-masking technology. Instead of eliminating bias from the recruiting process, it's making leaders biased toward the process itself. One of these leaders summed it up this way: "I wish my company would stop treating me like I'm a member of a hate group. I don't care who the candidate is, where they go to church, or their socioeconomic status. Which box they check for ethnicity is irrelevant. So is the fact that they may identify with the letters in LGBTQ. None of that matters. I care about one thing . . . can they do the work?"

What these organizations lack is durable diversity. Durable diversity creates a dependable workforce of complementary people. Organizations that are durably diverse look at the whole person when hiring. Their leaders recognize that each individual is more than a title, skillset, or member of an ethnic group. They're not colorblind or gender neutral. Just the opposite. They're hyperaware that maintaining a diverse and dependable workforce requires being able to select from a robust flow of different types of people.

If you've done business with the world's most admired companies, you've experienced the benefits of durable diversity. Drop into a Starbucks. Go to the Apple store. Visit a Disney theme park. Note the diversity of their people. We love these companies because of these people. The rich tapestry of their backgrounds, skills, and experiences supports them in creating superior products and services.

You might be thinking that your company is different—that your organization lacks the brand recognition or reputation to draw in such a highly qualified diverse workforce. Top organizations didn't start out as household names. They became well known because they chose a well-rounded group of employees that did excellent work. Work that made their companies great.

The Talent Accelerator Process will help you achieve durable diversity. The first five steps of TAP allow you to enrich, harness, and sustain a dependable workforce of complementary people.

Step #1: Create Hire-Right Profiles

Hire-Right Profiles can be a catalyst for diversity. Does this mean you add gender, race, or other differentiators as Dealmakers? No. To do so would prejudice your hiring. Tapping into a wider, diverse candidate base often only requires recategorizing hiring criteria.

The simple act of adjusting one Dealmaker is how a mortgage bank got on the path to durable diversity. For years, the bank had a reputation for being "blindingly white." The executive team knew of this reputation and made creating a diverse workforce a key strategic initiative. They read lots of books, passing on ideas they'd gleaned to the management team. Members of the HR staff were sent to conferences on diversity, with hopes they'd learn new ideas. Budgets were increased, expanding the head-count of corporate recruiters. Yet, the lack of diversity remained a painful issue. The search for a solution went on.

The bank eventually gave the Talent Accelerator Process a try. They followed the steps, in order, beginning with creating Hire-Right Profiles for their core roles. This had an immediate payoff. A manager noticed that a four-year degree in finance showed up as a Dealmaker for each role. He challenged this idea, asking his colleagues why this was a required attribute. Initially, there was lots of pushback. A finance degree had been an employment requirement for these core roles for years. He kept at it, asking if anyone had proof that this was absolutely necessary for someone to succeed at the bank. The room got quiet. No one could offer a shred of evidence that a finance degree should be a Dealmaker.

Having a bachelor's degree in finance was recategorized as a Boost. Now, recruiters could reach out to people with all types of college degrees, including associate and bachelor's degrees in any field of study. Changing this one Dealmaker created flexibility as they leveraged each of the talent streams. The floodgates of the local talent pool spilled open, delivering a deluge of diverse well-qualified candidates.

It's normal to put everything but the kitchen sink in your Dealmakers. Having an overly restrictive list of Dealbreakers is common as well. One or more of your criteria in either quadrant could block the flow of diverse top talent.

Take some time to review each item in the top half of a Hire-Right Profile. Ideally, you'll do this with your hiring team, making it a dialogue. Challenge any assumptions you hear. Push back if someone says, "But this is how it's always been done." Be willing to compromise by suggesting that you experiment with two different versions of the Hire-Right Profile during the next round of hiring.

Here are some questions to discuss as you consider each Dealmaker and Dealbreaker:

- Why is this Dealmaker/Dealbreaker important?

- What proof do we have that it's necessary?

- Who have we promoted internally that didn't match those criteria? Have they succeeded in that role? If so, what does this tell us about it being a requirement?

- What alternatives are there to those criteria? Which other types of degrees could suffice? How about on-the-job training? What about transferable skills?

Step #2: Improve Candidate Gravity

Increasing your pull on talent can broaden your access to a diverse candidate base. Job ads and posts on social media can target an expanded audience. An applicant tracking system can be mined for candidates who weren't previously seen as a fit. You can request additional referrals, attend new networking events, and ask external talent scouts to broaden their search. You can also create talent. That's what an IT company in India did to build a diverse workforce.

For years, the company had difficulty finding enough qualified people to fill all the jobs in their network operations center (NOC). The NOC operated 24 hours a day, seven days a week. Each work shift required hundreds of employees for things to run smoothly. Recruiting enough talent had always been a challenge. Changes in technology prompted frequent changes in their hiring profile. Many candidates lacked the new skills the company was seeking.

The managing director, who had primary responsibility over hiring, was a fan of candidate gravity. In particular, he liked the idea that talent could be manufactured. He saw this as a solution to his people shortage, and it would allow him to create greater diversity in the NOC.

Across the globe, diversity means different things. In India, diversity runs wide and deep. The country has 22 official languages, plus hundreds of dialects. There are several major religions, thousands of tribes, and a system of castes and sub-castes. These differences have polarized people into groups who have little in common, and even less contact with one another. The NOC's managing director saw this as an opportunity, not an obstacle. The rich diversity of his country meant there were lots of pools of untapped talent.

Hire-Right Profiles were pared down to essential skills and then shared companywide. The company had offices throughout the country. These offices employed a vast cross-section of Indian society. Employees were asked to tap into their unique communities to uncover prospective talent. Candidates who had essential skills were interviewed, and hired if they were a good fit. As new employees, they were taught the new skills needed in their jobs.

This initiative was successful for several reasons. The company tapped into often overlooked candidates that could fill jobs and improve the diversity of the workforce. New hires became loyal employees, grateful that the company was willing to expand their work experience. Plus, internal employees in non-IT roles began applying for jobs at the NOC. The pared-down Hire-Right Profiles opened the door for these workers to transfer between departments.

Manufacturing a diverse group of workers for your company starts with your hiring profile. When you reevaluate which skills are essential versus teachable, you expand the possibilities for who may be a fit. Prospective candidates, internal or external, can then be hired for an open role and "skilled" into becoming productive employees. How you do that depends on the individual:

- **Upskill:** A worker with the basic aptitude for a role, but lacking specific skills, can be upskilled. For instance, let's say you're looking for a head chef for a restaurant. You've tried tapping into a diverse pool of talent, but many people lack experience in managing the business side of a kitchen. So, you focus your search on people with excellent culinary skills. Once hired, you upskill your new chef by sending him or her to some business classes.

- **Reskill:** A candidate could have a solid work history, but it's in a different industry. Reskilling could turn that individual into a great employee. John retired after 30 years of working for a county agency, pushing lots of paper in an administrative role. Yet, he was good with his hands, tinkering with projects around the house. A plumbing company saw potential and helped John reskill so he could do a different job than he was used to.

Step #3: Maximize Hiring Styles

Selecting employees is easier when you have a hiring team. Your combined perceptions will counter hiring blindness. The team can also keep bias in check. That was the case for Team TalentSeeker. Their unified approach to hiring helped them build a diverse accounting department.

The four people comprising Team TalentSeeker took their responsibilities seriously. Thus the name they bestowed upon themselves. They spent every workday managing financial matters for their corporate office, and only wanted the best people around them.

One round of interviews forever changed their perspectives on diversity. Prior to these interviews, every member of the team believed themselves unbiased: That they made their hiring choices based upon someone's ability to do a job, not because of gender, race, or other diversity dimension.

In discussing the four candidates they'd interviewed, three members of the hiring team thought one candidate, in particular, was the best one. She perfectly matched the top half of the Hire-Right Profile. Plus, they'd checked off several Boosts, including that she spoke three different languages.

The fourth member of the group, Bart, wasn't sold. His teammates asked questions, trying to understand his concerns. He tried to articulate his reasons but struggled to explain himself. This went on for 20 minutes. Out of frustration, one of the team members in favor of hiring the candidate said, "She's different from everyone else we've hired. Might your concern be her race? Maybe her gender?"

The room got quiet. No one had ever challenged another team member in this way. Then Bart said, "Initially, I was going to tell you that wasn't the case. In fact, had I responded immediately, I would've shouted that gender and race have nothing to do with it. Your question made me that angry. However, as I thought about it, I realized I wasn't angry with you. I was mad at myself after I recognized that race and gender are exactly why I'm hesitant to hire her."

Bart's admission began an intimate conversation about the nature of bias. "I was thinking how different she is from the rest of the team," said Bart. "Wondering how she'd fit in. Worrying that hiring her may not work out because of racial differences. I wasn't intending to act in a biased way. But that's exactly what I was doing." Bart's honesty invited others to openly share. Each team member gave examples of how they'd behaved prejudicially in the past, much of it unintentional. Right then and there, they made a commitment to watch closely for bias.

Bias can be cunning. Like Bart, we can have the best intentions, but those intentions end up unintentionally prejudicing our decisions. Your hiring team can help avert this when you do two things:

1. **Stay connected:** The members of Team TalentSeeker trusted one another. That trust was built and nurtured through the strong connection they maintained. Staying connected with your hiring team builds rapport, making it easier to spot and communicate behaviors that could be rooted in bias.

2. **Stay honest:** Make a pact to be honest with your teammates about any form of bias. Discuss how to best communicate this if it shows up. Then, point bias out when you see it. Just remember to say what you mean without saying it mean.

Step #4: Conduct Experiential Interviews

Seeing someone do quality work makes it easier to judge the work instead of the person. That's why hands-on interviews are a powerful tool in combating prejudicial hiring.

I discovered the extent of this power when faced with a challenging client—one that I considered "firing." Their manufacturing plant was one of the most discriminatory environments I'd ever experienced.

Witnessing blatant discrimination was nothing new. Some prospective customers of my recruiting services voiced gender and racial preferences in job candidates. I'd firmly state that I didn't work that way, and we'd go our separate ways. As an executive, I had to counsel managers on potentially discriminatory employment practices. In consulting, I've had to point out illegal hiring methods, ending relationships when organizations refused to clean up their act. Which is why I considered ending my consulting engagement with that manufacturer. I doubted they'd change their ways.

What was the problem? Hiring bias was the rule, not the exception. The plant operated in a caste-like system. Preferences for several ethnicities were openly stated for assembly line workers. These ethnicities were supposedly hard workers. Supervisors were next in the hierarchy, chosen from one particular race. Jobs in management were filled exclusively with men. Discrimination was rampant, infusing itself into the company's DNA. Changing this appeared daunting, maybe even impossible.

However, I saw things through. Why? Because of one person—the production manager. He'd joined the manufacturer earlier that year, coming from another plant in town. There, he'd had a diverse workforce and knew the benefits of hiring all types of people. He'd accepted this new job knowing he'd have his work cut out for him.

His belief in the people he worked with is what convinced me to stay. "They're not bad people," he said. "They're good folks who're making poor choices. We used the Talent Accelerator Process at my last employer. I know we can use it to help them stop our prejudicial hiring practices."

In particular, he saw experiential interviews as his primary instrument for changing perspectives. "It's easy to judge a book by its cover," he said. "When you look further, you often find out your first reaction was incorrect. That's why hands-on interviews will make us successful. Hiring managers will see that their pre-conceived notions have been dead wrong."

Experiential interviews were initially rolled out in one department. The production manager made sure a diverse group of qualified candidates were considered during hands-on interviews. Hiring managers got to experience these candidates doing sample work. Then, they discussed whom they thought they should hire.

Not surprisingly, managers leaned toward "the usual suspects"—the candidates whose ethnicity fit the rest of the department. We'd anticipated this. The production manager knew exactly what to say. "You know what," he said, "having watched these candidates in action during their interviews, that was my first thought as well. And why wouldn't it be? We're used to hiring people who look and act like the rest of our staff. But when I compare the sample work done by each, some of the other candidates appear to be a better fit."

The hiring team discussed this idea—that it's normal to gravitate to what's familiar. All agreed this happened often in their lives, and that this may have influenced their initial reactions about the candidates. The further they looked, the clearer it became that this was true. Comparing how candidates per-formed in the hands-on interviews to the Hire-Right Profile sealed the deal. Only one of their new hires matched the dom-inant ethnicity of the department. The remainder came from a mixture of backgrounds. All were chosen because they were the best fit.

The production manager went on to incorporate experiential interviews throughout the plant. Over time, the manufacturer became more diverse. It didn't happen overnight. Some areas were slower to adapt than others. However, diversity, not dis-crimination, became the standard. Jobs were filled quickly, because they were tapping into a wider and deeper pool of talent.

Our thinking can be tricky. Without realizing it, our persistent thoughts can become deep ruts. These ruts narrow our perspec-tive of how we view the world. That's why our first thought about something can seem like a conditioned response. We're stuck in that rut, that mindset. That's what happened at the manufacturer. They were stuck in their persistent way of thinking about who would fit and who would not.

Does this behavior excuse bias? No, of course not. But it does explain it, and shows us what we need to do differently. We're not responsible for our first thought, but we are responsible for our next action. That's how the manufacturer started building a diverse workforce. They didn't just go with their first thoughts about candidates. They challenged that mindset, looking at how people performed the tasks they were given in hands-on inter-views. After a while, they found that their thinking started to change, and those old prejudicial ruts disappeared.

Experiential interviewing is a powerful tool in combating discrimination—much better than blind hiring. Blind hiring doesn't address why bias happens. Experiential interviewing does.

It helps organizations hire fairly, while also impacting how hiring managers think and act.

Step #5: Maintain a Talent Inventory

Earlier in the book, I shared that readily accessible inventories of talent provide shared benefits—the inventory advantage. Candidates get to line up better jobs. You have people ready to hire, when they're needed. You might expect that the first four steps of the Talent Accelerator Process are the most important for sustaining durable diversity. That's true, as long as you stay in regular contact with prospective hires in your Talent Inventory. The benefits of your Talent Inventory can also be shared with colleagues both inside and outside of your organization to help them maintain a diverse workforce.

A good example of helping internal colleagues occurred at a telecom company. Several locations were more successful than others at building inventories of diverse talent. A senior executive noticed this and laid out a mandate that locations start sharing their Talent Inventories. How was this received? Initially, not well. Leaders at locations with large inventories of talent took offense. They'd worked hard to build pools of prospective employees. Also, not everyone in an inventory would be willing to consider a job in a different location.

How'd the telecom company work out these issues? They helped all parties get their needs met. Money played a big part. Signing bonuses were offered to candidates if they moved to a different city. Company locations were financially compensated when candidates from their inventory were hired by another office. Did this make everyone happy? It did. Candidates were accepting offers. Locations supplying that talent received much needed budget dollars.

The same idea works between different organizations. Even competitors. You may find this surprising. Why would competitors want to share their most important asset—talent? It's simple. It starts with mindset.

Competition is healthy. It's a sign that an industry is viable, creating enough business opportunities for everyone. Competitors who view the world in this manner and also believe in the importance of diversity are frequently open to talent-sharing agreements. These agreements vary. This could include compensating another organization when you hire from their inventory. It also could include "borrowing" talent, keeping individuals working until needed by the organization that originally found them.

You get to choose how you leverage the advantages gained by your Talent Inventory. Maintaining a diverse pool of people gives you lots of options, including the option to share talent with others.

Collective Wisdom

I grew up watching reruns of the original *Star Trek* TV series. As the *Star Trek* franchise expanded, so too did my interest in it. The next installment in the franchise was called *Star Trek: The Next Generation*. This new series was filled with a universe of bad guys. One of them, however, stood out above the others—the nasty alien race known as the Borg. Part humanoid, part android, the Borg swelled their ranks by assimilating humans into their fold. Each addition became part of a linked group of minds that worked together, making them a formidable enemy.

(continued)

As an adult, I've thought about the Borg. What if they'd used their collective knowledge for good? What problems could they have solved? How could they have made the universe a better place? As I thought about it, I realized we've experienced this kind of good already. It was happening every day in companies with a diverse workforce.

There's tremendous power within a unified group of diverse people working together to do good. The group benefits from collective wisdom. Their diverse backgrounds allow them to use their varying knowledge and experiences to seize opportunities and tackle problems. They're more powerful than a supercomputer, efficiently processing information and generating unique ideas and solutions.

Does this mean that companies without a diverse workforce are like *Star Trek* villains? Of course not. Collective wisdom is the reason behind the better financial results of the most diverse companies. It's also why diverse leadership teams are helping their organizations outpace competitors.

I shared these thoughts with Dr. Jeff Pon, SHRM's chief human resources and strategy officer. Having grown up around the same time, he was familiar with *Star Trek*. He acknowledged that a diverse workforce can give an organization a competitive edge. "Diversity brings together more perspectives," said Pon. "Tapping into these perspectives gives an organization better information, information that can be used to improve their performance."

Pon went on to explain why collective wisdom is especially important today. "How work gets done is changing," Pon said, "and will continue to change. Leaders have to leverage smart ideas both inside and outside their organization. Doing so helps them remain adaptive and competitive. A diverse organization is naturally equipped to do this, given its propensity toward being open to differing perspectives."

Pon's role at SHRM, along with a successful career as an HR executive prior to joining the association, has allowed him to observe many diversity initiatives. I asked him why some succeed and others fail.

(continued)

"Diversity succeeds when an organization has a strong infrastructure to support it," said Pon. "This includes aligning diversity initiatives with the organization's core values, and supporting it with an effective recruiting process and talent pipeline. A successful organization also remains grounded in why diversity matters. Its leaders believe that diversity demonstrates fairness and morality, gives the organization access to a broader range of skills and backgrounds, and identifies new sources of talent to better serve customers."

"When diversity initiatives fail," Pon said, "it's usually for several reasons. Our research at SHRM shows that the main barrier to diversity and inclusion initiatives is internal resistance to changing policies and practices. Diversity initiatives are also likely to fail when organizations incorporate taboo ideas like hiring quotas. Quotas can raise concerns about discrimination against people from mainstream groups. Diversity and inclusion programs also tend to fail when they are poorly defined. Diversity needs to be adjusted to the local context. Apart from gender, which seems to be a universal issue, organizations need to find the diversity dimensions that are important and relevant in their specific region."

In wrapping up his insights, Pon referred back to *Star Trek*. He pointed out that Spock, one of the main characters in the original series, would bid farewell by saying, "Live long and prosper." "That's what happens when you tap into the collective wisdom of a diverse workforce," he said. "You're increasing your organization's ability to succeed, improving the likelihood that it will prosper for a long time."

Healing Divisiveness

In newspapers and on TV, the world appears divisive: More than I've ever experienced in my lifetime. Politicians point out that the opposing party is out to get us. Specific countries are viewed as a threat to global security. Race continues to play a role in confrontations between citizens and police. Sexual harassment in the workplace and in schools seems rampant. It's easy to feel powerless over these problems.

Can we do something to heal this divisiveness? We can, by exerting the power we do have. One of those powers is hiring. Improving diversity in hiring won't cure divisiveness, but it can put a healthy dent in it. Why? Because of the importance of work. We spend a large chunk of each week at our jobs. Those hours impact how we think and the ways in which we act. We carry that home with us, impacting our family, friends, and communities.

This is one of the beautiful things about diversity in the workplace—its impact on society. I've seen countless examples of how a diverse workforce can influence positive change beyond the workplace.

One example, in particular, stands out. A pair of workers from a diverse organization lived in the same neighborhood, a neighborhood rife with crime. Neighbors blamed one another, focusing on racial differences and believing that these differences were the root cause of the crime problems.

The workers from the diverse organization stepped up, using communication and collaboration skills they'd acquired working with colleagues. They used these skills to tear down baseless accusations and build trust. They also helped create a neighborhood watch program to actively monitor activities.

In a short time, crime decreased dramatically. Just as important, new friendships were formed that, a few months before, would have seemed impossible. Neighbors still credit the pair of workers for being the catalyst for this change.

Action List for Chapter 11

The Talent Accelerator Process will help you maintain a diverse workforce when you take the steps that follow.

Discuss the Importance of Diversity

Does diversity matter to everyone in your organization? Possibly not. Bad experiences with diversity initiatives are common. Leaders who've had these negative experiences may believe in diversity, but not the hiring practices that were associated with it. Have an open discussion about the importance of a diverse workforce. Focus the conversation on how companies achieve diversity, and the pros and cons of different initiatives. Taking this approach solicits honest opinions, versus political correctness. The insights you gain will help you shape how you tackle your organization's diversity challenges.

Assess the Durability of Your Diversity and Inclusion Initiatives

Are your diversity initiatives working? Why? Why not? Incorporate what's working into your Talent Accelerator Process. Replace what's not with ideas from this book.

Use the first five steps of the Talent Accelerator Process to address specific problems. As an example, let's say you notice that diversity isn't improving in a department. You determine that there's an adequate flow of diverse talent making it to interviews. These interviews are producing potential hires from a single ethnicity. This narrows the problem down to the interview, showing you where to address the issue.

Share Successes

It's hard to argue with success. Share the successes of your diversity and inclusion initiatives. Point out how a diverse workforce has improved customer satisfaction or financial results. Sharing these details may not win over the hearts and minds of bigots. Success can, however, show open-minded leaders who've had bad experiences with diversity that your approach is different.

Access the Collective Wisdom in Your Community

Professional organizations provide access to valuable research and ideas on diversity. For example, SHRM has surveyed members who are on diversity's front lines. The organization's *Global Diversity and Inclusion* report details their findings, including how the most successful diversity initiatives are supported by an organization's most senior leaders.

In Appendix D, you'll find links to organizations that offer important updates on diversity.

A Rising Tide of Talent

Opportunities for advancement are important, especially to top talent. They're driven to achieve and desire recognition for their contributions. One of the ways they receive recognition is through advancement. Promotions provide proof that they're valued by your organization, and give them an opportunity to take on new challenges.

Without clear advancement opportunities, your best employees could believe they'll be forever stuck in their current roles. Seeing no way to climb up your org chart, they'll leap into other jobs outside your company. That's why a lack of advancement opportunities is a frequent cause of employee turnover.

Designing a career path is but one part of advancing employees' careers. Another important part is often completely avoided because of its perceived risk. I learned about this "risk" early in my career.

Every year our company had an annual meeting. At the end of our two days together, it was tradition to have a Q&A session. Our CEO and his executive team sat at the front of room, answering our questions. Any topic was fair game.

I'd been thinking about my question for a while. I was a rising star, and was hoping to rise even faster. My question for the CEO: "How can I get on the fast track for promotion?" In his usual succinct fashion, he said, "That's easy. Make yourself expendable."

A deep silence descended over the room. As I looked around, I saw looks of horror on many faces. A few of my colleagues shot dirty looks my way, seeming to imply that I'd somehow caused harm in posing my question.

The CEO could see our discomfort. "I get it," he said. "That's an unsettling thing to hear. I was given the same answer when I was starting out in my own career. It made me squirm. However, that's the reality. We can't promote anyone who we still need in their current role."

Many people remain stuck in their current jobs because they're the only ones who can do that job. They can't advance, even when there's a career path for them. They can't step up because there's no one to take their place.

High Velocity Hiring fixes this problem by creating a rising tide of talent. Instead of succession plans that fail for lack of qualified successors, the continuous influx of top talent expedites advancement and elevates careers.

Your Talent Accelerator Process can propel your best employees up the org chart. This starts with your Hire-Right Profile. As you create Hire-Right Profiles, remain mindful about succession planning. Include traits, either as Dealmakers or Boosts, that will make new hires promotable. Using these profiles in each subsequent step of TAP ensures your organization can promote more often from within.

Will some employees still fail to make themselves expendable? Yes, but less often. Especially when you communicate your organization's commitment to creating a rising tide of talent; and then, backing that up with a steady flow of quality employees that keep seats filled.

Many of the organizations that use the Talent Accelerator Process say it closes the loop. Instead of having to constantly look outside the organization for candidates, they look more often within. Their employees become an inventory of promotable people, giving them the ultimate stream of top talent—their own employees.

A rising tide of talent is but one of many ongoing benefits you'll experience in using the Talent Accelerator Process. TAP will help you create your own ecosystem of powerful people who do quality work. Participating in the new way of hiring will give your organization an edge over competitors who remain stuck in the slow lane of hiring. Continued use of TAP will allow you to maintain a diverse Talent Inventory of exceptional employees who propel you into the future. A future filled with expanded opportunities. All because you've committed to being able to hire in an instant.

APPENDIX A
Internet Links

Throughout the book I've provided links to a variety of resources. It's likely some of those links will change over time. To help with that, I'll check them from time to time and publish updates, when available, on the Wintrip Consulting Group website. Also on the website, you'll find additional *High Velocity Hiring* resources. Here's the link to that page:

resources.highvelocityhiring.com

Recommended Assets for Hire-Right Profiles

The following Dealmakers, listed by type of role, are often overlooked by organizations. Candidates who've had these assets have gone on to be top employees.

Administrative Support

Asset: Respectful Pushback

There are lots of "yes" people—individuals who'll tell you what you want to hear. Not an ideal trait for someone in an administrative support role. Candidates who respectfully push back don't let important details slide. They'll give honest feedback that helps you do better work.

Accounting

Asset: Expedient Accuracy

Thoroughness should rule the day in accounting, but not at the expense of expediency. Delays in processing payments, generating reports, analyzing financials, and other accounting functions can undermine your business. Candidates with expedient accuracy are able to balance accuracy and speed.

Construction

Asset: Preventive Mindset

Many repairs are preventable, especially when you hire candidates for construction roles who have a preventive mindset. They look ahead, seeing the ramifications of their work before it's completed. They'll push for adjustments to projects that make it better, preventing future problems.

Creative

Asset: Practical Creativity

There are lots of brilliant people in creative roles. As they design products, artwork, digital media, and other creative works, the best of the lot strive for practicality. They understand that users of their work benefit most when they balance creativity with practical simplicity.

Education

Asset: Progressive Continuity

The ideas, tools, and media available to educators are growing exponentially. Educators with the progressive continuity asset keep what works and evolve the rest. They stay grounded in sound teaching practices while incorporating new technologies and methods.

Engineering

Asset: Global Precision

Engineering roles combine big-picture thinking and small-detail responsibility. When projects are delayed or have cost overruns, it's usually because someone lost sight of the big picture or missed small details. Hiring engineering professionals with the global precision asset eliminates these problems.

Government

Asset: Bureaucratic Hospitality

Governmental agencies are often criticized because of the people who work there. They're accused of being rude, incompetent, or lacking a sense of urgency. Agencies that hire people with bureaucratic hospitality achieve better outcomes. Their work is done efficiently and competently while treating citizens with warmth and respect.

Healthcare

Asset: Pragmatic Communication

Medical terminology can be intimidating when you're well. The stress of injury or illness makes it overwhelming when you're a patient or family members making important decisions. Healthcare facilities that hire people with the pragmatic communication asset create a different experience. They distill medical jargon into easily understandable ideas, helping patients and families make informed choices.

Hospitality

Asset: Anticipatory Service

The best way to solve a problem is to never let it happen. The ideal way to delight a customer is to provide something before they ask. Hospitality professionals with the anticipatory service asset do both. Regardless of their area of work, they deliver distinct and memorable service because they think and act ahead.

Information Technology

Asset: Fail-Safe Mentality

Much of our world relies on technology. When it fails, things come to a screeching halt. That's why hiring IT pros with a fail-safe mentality is important, especially those who plan and design technology. They do their best to make tech foolproof, but don't stop there. They incorporate redundancies that kick in if primary systems go awry, helping ensure that core functions keep running.

Legal

Asset: Succinct Thoroughness

There's a new breed of legal professional. They develop thorough and concise legal documents. These documents contain language that's easy to understand. They have the succinct thoroughness asset, which drives them to do comprehensive and precise work without sacrificing simplicity.

Public Safety

Asset: Compassionate Authority

Life-saving roles, such as police officers, firefighters, and EMTs, are challenging and important. Each role comes with a high level of authority. Sometimes, authority can go to someone's head. Not so with candidates who have the compassionate authority asset. They're fair and firm, never letting the weight of their authority overshadow the compassion in their hearts.

Research

Asset: Balanced Passion

All work and no play make life dull. Too much work can also dull the capabilities of those in research. Candidates for research roles with the balanced passion asset recognize the importance of time off. Time off allows their subconscious minds to process information in the background. When they return to work, they're refreshed and full of new thoughts and ideas.

Retail

Asset: Respectful Attentiveness

Shoppers don't want to be stalked by a retail associate or store manager. They desire space to browse without pressure, knowing that there's someone available to help when needed. Retail staff with respectful attentiveness provide this experience. They're present, not pushy. Shoppers trust them and are inclined to buy from them.

Resources for Finding Staffing Providers

In Chapter 10, I recommended picking a staffing partner that's a member of a reputable association. Below is a list of such associations. Those included provide access to their member lists and require members to abide by a code of standards. You can read more about each association's standards on their websites. Associations are listed under the country of their headquarters.

Australia and New Zealand

Information Technology Contract and Recruitment Association Ltd (ITCRA)
   www.itcra.com

Recruitment & Consulting Services Association (RCSA)
   www.rcsa.com.au

Canada

The Association of Canadian Search, Employment and Staffing
Services (ACSESS)
www.acsess.org

China

China Association of Foreign Service Trades (CAFST)
www.cafst.org.cn

France

Prism'emploi—Professionnels du recrutement et de l'intérim
www.prismemploi.eu

Germany

Association of Professional Staffing Companies (APSCo Germany)
www.apsco.org/international/apsco-germany.aspx

India

Indian Staffing Federation
www.indianstaffingfederation.org

Japan

Japan Staffing Services Association
www.jassa.jp

Mexico

Asociación Mexicana de Empresas de Capital Humano (AMECH)
www.amech.com.mx

Philippines

Philippine Association of Local Service Contractors (PALSCON)
www.palscon.org

Russia

The Association of Private Employment Agencies
www.achaz.ru

Singapore

Association of Professional Staffing Companies (APSCo Asia)
www.apsco.org/asia/apsco-asia.aspx

South Africa

The Federation of African Professional Staffing Organisations (APSO)
www.apso.co.za

South Korea

Korea HR Services Industry Association
www.kostaffs.or.kr

United Kingdom

Association of Professional Staffing Companies (APSCo)
www.apsco.org

Recruitment & Employment Confederation (REC)
www.rec.uk.com

United States

American Staffing Association
www.americanstaffing.net

Association of Executive Search and Leadership Consultants
www.aesc.org

National Association of Locum Tenens Organizations
www.nalto.org

National Association of Personnel Services (NAPS)
www.naps360.org

TechServe Alliance
www.techservealliance.org

Global

World Employment Confederation (WEC)
Members of WEC include national associations across the globe.
Links to these associations can be found in their membership
section.
www.wecglobal.org

Diversity and Inclusion Resources

If you're looking for additional resources, I've listed a handful of organizations below that make diversity at least part of their focus. Descriptions of each organization were taken directly from their websites.

Council for Global Immigration (CFGI)

CFGI aims to provide the resources and support necessary to advance employment-based immigration of highly educated professionals worldwide.

www.cfgi.org

The Equal Employment Advisory Council (EEAC)

EEAC is a nonprofit employer association that provides guidance to its member companies on understanding and complying with their Equal Employment Opportunity and affirmative action obligations.

www.eeac.org

National Diversity Council (NDC)

NDC is a nonpartisan organization dedicated to being both a resource and an advocate for the value of diversity and inclusion.

www.nationaldiversitycouncil.org

Society for Human Resource Management (SHRM)

SHRM is the world's largest HR professional society, representing 285,000 members in more than 165 countries.

www.shrm.org

World Federation of People Management Associations (WFPMA)

WFPMA is an organization representing more than 600,000 people management professionals in over 90 national personnel associations around the world.

www.wfpma.com

NOTES

Introduction

1. *Fortune*, "World's Most Admired Companies," accessed July 22, 2016, http://fortune.com/worlds-most-admired-companies/.
2. PTI, "A Bad Hire Can Cost 5 Times His Annual Salary to a Firm: Report," http://articles.economictimes.indiatimes.com/2015-05-25/news/62624552_1_bad-hire-annual-salary-organisation, *The Economic Times* (India), May 25, 2015.
3. PR Newswire, "Robert Half Survey: Executives Say Poor Skills Fit Most Common Reason New Hires Don't Work Out," news release, September 29, 2011, http://www.prnewswire.com/news-releases/robert-half-survey-executives-say-poor-skills-fit-most-common-reason-new-hires-dont-work-out-130770988.html.
4. DHI Hiring Indicators, accessed May 26, 2016, http://dhihiring indicators.com/.
5. U.S. Bureau of Labor Statistics, "Job Openings and Labor Turnover Summary," news release, May 10, 2016, http://www.bls.gov/news.release/archives/jolts_05102016.htm.
6. Jimmy John's website, accessed May 26, 2016, https://www.jimmyjohns.com/about-us/our-owner-founder/.
7. *Entrepreneur*, "2016 Top Franchises from Entrepreneur's Franchise 500 List," accessed December 8, 2016, http://www.entrepreneur.com/franchise500.

Chapter 1

1. Ben Rooney, "Big Data's Big Problem: Little Talent," http://www.wsj.com/articles/SB10001424052702304723304577365700368073674, *The Wall Street Journal*, April 29, 2012.
2. Joshua Wright, "America's Skilled Trades Dilemma: Shortages Loom As Most-In-Demand Group of Workers Age," *Forbes*, March 7, 2013, http://www.forbes.com/sites/emsi/2013/03/07/americas-skilled-trades-dilemma-shortages-loom-as-most-in-demand-group-of-workers-ages/#1b82a4234545.

3. Martha C. White, "These Are the Jobs Employers Are Desperate to Fill," *Time*, June 3, 2014, http://time.com/2814426/these-are -the-jobs-employers-are-desperate-to-fill/.

4. Judith Evans, "Skills Shortage Slows Housebuilding in the UK," https://www.ft.com/content/e52b0a22-b45e-11e5-8358-9a82b43f6b2f, *Financial Times*, January 6, 2016.

5. Matt Ferguson, "Employers Struggle to Find Skilled Workers," CNN, October 29, 2008, http://www.cnn.com/2008/LIVING/worklife/10/29/ cb.job.seekers.employers/index.html?iref=24hours.

6. Martin Fackler, "High-Tech Japan Running Out of Engineers," http:// www.nytimes.com/2008/05/17/business/worldbusiness/17engineers .html?_r=0, *The New York Times*, May 17, 2008.

7. Simon Santow, "Lawyer Shortage Despite Downturn," ABC, January 27, 2009, http://www.abc.net.au/worldtoday/content/2008/s2475203.htm.

8. Gouri Agtey Athale, "Skills Shortage Is the Biggest Concern in Auto Industry," http://articles.economictimes.indiatimes.com /2008-05-15/news/27733692_1_automotive-industry-design -engineering-automotive-companies, *The Economic Times* (India), May 15, 2008.

9. Simon McGee, "The Great Sheep Shearer Shortage: Hundreds Kept Out of Britain Because of New Visa Test," http://www.dailymail.co.uk/ news/article-1169369/The-great-sheep-shearer-shortage-hundreds -kept-Britain-new-visa-test.html, *The Mail on Sunday* (UK), April 11, 2009.

10. Staffing Industry Analysts, *North American Contingent Buyers Report*, December 10, 2015.

11. Barbara L. Fredrickson, Michael A. Cohn, Kimberly A. Coffey, Jolynn Pek, and Sandra M. Finkel, "Open Hearts Build Lives: Positive Emotions, Induced Through Loving-Kindness Meditation, Build Consequential Personal Resources," *Journal of Personality and Social Psychology*, no. 95.5 (2008): 1045–1062, http://www.ncbi.nlm.nih.gov/ pmc/articles/PMC3156028/?report=reader.

12. Ibid.

13. CareerBuilder.com, *Talentstream Supply and Demand Report* (Chicago, IL: CareerBuilder, March 24, 2016).

14. ManpowerGroup, *2015 Talent Shortage Survey* (Milwaukee, WI: ManpowerGroup, 2015), http://www.manpowergroup.com/wps/ wcm/connect/db23c560-08b6-485f-9bf6-f5f38a43c76a/2015_Talent_ Shortage_Survey_US-lo_res.pdf?MOD=AJPERES, 5.

Chapter 2

1. Brad Stone, *The Everything Store: Jeff Bezos and the Age of Amazon* (Boston: Little, Brown and Company, 2013), 294–295.
2. Ibid., 85.
3. Ibid., 88.
4. Amazon.com website, accessed May 27, 2016, https://www.amazon .com/dashbutton.
5. Brad Stone, *The Everything Store: Jeff Bezos and the Age of Amazon* (Boston: Little, Brown and Company, 2013), 294–295.
6. Netflix website, accessed May 27, 2016, http://ir.netflix.com/.
7. Upwork website, accessed December 13, 2016, https://www.upwork .com/about/.
8. Eric Houwen, "What We Did When Our Reqs Went from 80 to 400," *ERE*, April 29, 2015, http://www.eremedia.com/ere/what-we -did-when-our-reqs-went-from-80-to-400/.

Chapter 3

1. Jennifer S. Lerner, Ye Li, Piercarlo Valdesolo, and Karim Kassam, "Emotion and Decision Making," *Annual Review of Psychology*, vol. 66 (2015): 799–823, http://scholar.harvard.edu/files/jenniferlerner/files/ annual_review_manuscript_june_16_final.final_.pdf.
2. Ibid.

Chapter 4

1. Max Planck Society website, accessed July 25, 2016, https://www.mpg .de/532681/pressRelease20060302.

Chapter 5

1. Selective Attention Test video, accessed December 8, 2016, Daniel Simons and Christopher Chabris, http://www.dansimons.com/videos .html (1999).
2. Daniel Simons and Christopher Chabris, *The Invisible Gorilla* (New York: Harmony Books, 2011), 6.
3. Ibid., 19–21.
4. Ibid., 27–29.
5. Ibid., 33.

Chapter 8

1. Tax Foundation, "Americans Will Spend 8.9 Billion Hours, $409 Billion Complying with U.S. Tax Code in 2016," news release, June 15, 2016. http://taxfoundation.org/article/americans-will-spend-89-billion -hours-409-billion-complying-us-tax-code-2016.

2. Donald Sull, Rebecca Homkes, and Charles Sull, "Why Strategy Execution Unravels—and What to Do About It," *Forbes*, March 2015, https://hbr.org/2015/03/why-strategy-execution-unravelsand -what-to-do-about-it.

Chapter 9

1. USA Network, "eps2.0_unm4sk-pt1.tc," *MR. ROBOT* video, 41:16, July 13, 2016, http://www.usanetwork.com/mrrobot/episode-guide/ season-2-episode-1-eps20unm4sk-pt1tc.

Chapter 10

1. Erin Hatton, "The Rise of the Permanent Temp Economy," http:// opinionator.blogs.nytimes.com/2013/01/26/the-rise-of-the-permanent -temp-economy/, *The New York Times*, January 26, 2016.
2. American Staffing Association website, accessed July 19, 2016, https://americanstaffing.net/staffing-research-data/fact-sheets -analysis-staffing-industry-trends/staffing-industry-statistics /#tab:tbs_nav_item_1.
3. World Employment Confederation website, accessed December 16, 2016, http://www.wecglobal.org/index.php?id=163.
4. CareerBuilder.com, *Opportunities in Staffing* (Chicago, IL: CareerBuilder and Inavero, 2015).
5. ManpowerGroup website, accessed December 16, 2016, http:// manpowergroup.com/talent-shortage-2016.

Chapter 11

1. Vivian Hunt, Dennis Layton, and Sara Prince, "Why Diversity Matters," *McKinsey&Company*, January 2015, http://www .mckinsey.com/business-functions/organization/our-insights/why -diversity-matters.
2. Ibid.
3. Sebastien Malo, "More Women Executives Mean More Profits, According to Study of 91 Countries," *Reuters*, February 8, 2016, http://www.reuters.com/article/us-employment-women -profit-idUSKCN0VI040.

INDEX

ABOUT THE AUTHOR

Scott Wintrip has changed how thousands of companies across the globe find and select employees, helping design and implement a process to hire top talent in less than an hour. Over the past 18 years, he built the Wintrip Consulting Group (Wintrip ConsultingGroup.com), a thriving global consultancy. Scott, the acknowledged leader of the on-demand hiring movement, is pioneering improved methods for recruiting and interviewing job candidates. For five consecutive years, Staffing Industry Analysts, a Crain Communications company, has awarded Scott a place on the "Staffing 100," a list of the world's 100 most influential staffing leaders. He's also a member of the Million Dollar Consultant Hall of Fame and was recently inducted into the Staffing 100 Hall of Fame. Scott and his wife, Holly, live in St. Petersburg, Florida.

SCOTT WINTRIP

Helping companies hire in an instant®

✔ Invite Scott to Speak

Scott's programs are consistently the highest rated sessions at conferences and corporate events. Why? He provides practical solutions, engaging audience members to think, laugh, and feel compelled to take action. Learn how to book Scott for your next event at ScottWintrip.com.

✔ Hire Scott as Your Advisor

Gain direct access to Scott and his expertise. Known for his timely advice and responsiveness, he's retained as an advisor by leaders across the globe. Visit ScottWintrip.com and choose the Services link to learn more.

✔ Join Scott's Community

Scott regularly shares his wisdom and wit in his articles, podcasts, editorial cartoons, and videos. Sign up for his newsletter and read his blog at ScottWintrip.com. Be sure to follow Scott on social media.

 scottwintrip

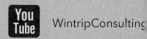 WintripConsulting